Lectora® 101: Ten Easy Steps for Beginners

This book explains step-by-step how to use Lectora 11 for people new to Lectora. It takes you through the steps you see below. Once you have applied this book to a course or two, if you find yourself using Lectora 5-10 hours a week, consider getting better by getting the follow-on books *Lectora 201: What They Don't Tell You in Class* and *Lectora 301: Techniques for Professionals*.

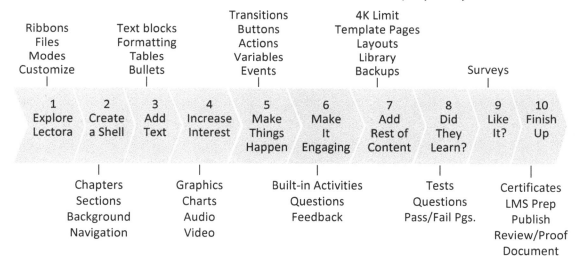

Books by the Author

Effective eLearning Design series:

> Vol. 1: Designing Effective eLearning: A Step-by-Step Guide
>
> Vol. 2: Superb eLearning using Low-Cost Scenarios: A Step-by-Step Guide to eLearning by Doing
>
> Vol. 3: ILT to CBT (hopefully 2015)

Mastering Lectora® series:

> Lectora 101: Ten Easy Steps for Beginners
>
> Lectora 201: What They Don't Tell You in Class
>
> Lectora 301: Techniques for Professionals
>
> Lectora Upgrade Guide (X to 11)

About the Author

Benjamin Pitman is a training and instructional design professional with over 20 years of experience. He is a Certified Internet Webmaster and holds a Ph.D. in Human Resource Development majoring in adult learning. He has been developing training for over 20 years and e-learning courses for over 10 years. He has helped thousands of people with Lectora problems on the community forum and is known there as "Dr. Lectora."

Ben would be glad to help you with designing e-learning as well as development in Lectora. Here is his contact information:

ben.pitman@eProficiency.com
678-571-4179 in Atlanta, GA
www.eProficiency.com

Lectora® 101:

Ten Easy Steps for Beginners

Edition 1.0

May 2013

Benjamin Pitman, Ph.D.
a.k.a. Dr. Lectora

eProficiency, Inc.
1810 Chattahoochee Run Drive
Suwanee, GA 30024
678-571-4179
www.eProficiency.com

For general information on other products and services including training and coaching, or technical support, please visit www.eProficiency.com or contact Benjamin Pitman at 678-571-4179, support@eProficiency.com.

Trademarks: Lectora is a registered trademark of Trivantis Corporation. Windows®, Microsoft®, Microsoft® Word®, and PowerPoint® are registered trademarks of Microsoft® Corporation. Flash® is a registered trademark of Adobe Systems Inc. Other product and company names mentioned herein may be the trademarks of their respective owners. Use of trademarks or product names is not intended to convey endorsement or affiliation with this book.

Library of Congress Cataloging-in-Publication Data

Pitman, Benjamin.

Lectora 101: Ten Easy Steps for Beginners

Includes bibliographical references and index.

ISBN-13: 978-1483960333

ISBN-10: 1483960331

1. Lectora. 2. Computer-based training development. 3. Authoring tools. 4. Authoring Applications. 5. Web-based training development.

To Emily, my daughter.

And Fred, my college roommate and friend
for over half a century, who helped me
keep my head straight as I wrote this book.

Thanks to all my clients, Jay Lambert, and
the Trivantis staff without whom this book
would not have been possible.

A special thanks to Ron Wincek and his
company who gave me a place to work
when home had too many distractions.

And of course, to my wife who supported
me through the dark days.

Contents

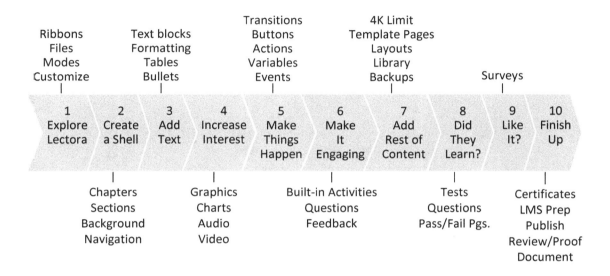

Ribbons
Files
Modes
Customize

Text blocks
Formatting
Tables
Bullets

Transitions
Buttons
Actions
Variables
Events

4K Limit
Template Pages
Layouts
Library
Backups

Surveys

| 1 Explore Lectora | 2 Create a Shell | 3 Add Text | 4 Increase Interest | 5 Make Things Happen | 6 Make It Engaging | 7 Add Rest of Content | 8 Did They Learn? | 9 Like It? | 10 Finish Up |

Chapters
Sections
Background
Navigation

Graphics
Charts
Audio
Video

Built-in Activities
Questions
Feedback

Tests
Questions
Pass/Fail Pgs.

Certificates
LMS Prep
Publish
Review/Proof
Document

Step 2: Create Your Course Shell—27

Step 3: Add and Format Text—45

Step 1: Learn Your Way Around Lectora

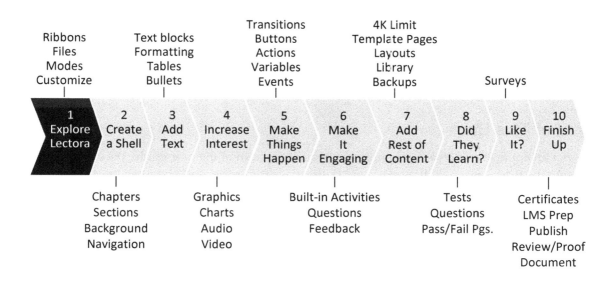

Ribbons Files Modes Customize	Text blocks Formatting Tables Bullets		Transitions Buttons Actions Variables Events			4K Limit Template Pages Layouts Library Backups			Surveys
1 Explore Lectora	2 Create a Shell	3 Add Text	4 Increase Interest	5 Make Things Happen	6 Make It Engaging	7 Add Rest of Content	8 Did They Learn?	9 Like It?	10 Finish Up
	Chapters Sections Background Navigation		Graphics Charts Audio Video		Built-in Activities Questions Feedback		Tests Questions Pass/Fail Pgs.		Certificates LMS Prep Publish Review/Proof Document

Above you see the 10 steps we will go through to get you started with Lectora. You should see some things that look very familiar from your work with PowerPoint®.

To get started, let's get familiar with Lectora.

Do a Reality Check	Before we get too far along, let's be sure this book is for you. Does the goal of this book fit with your goals? Are you okay with this book what this book does *not* cover? Do you have the right prerequisites?
Compare Power-Point® to Lectora	If you know PowerPoint®, you will want to read this section to see what is similar and what is different between the two.
Get to Know Lectora	Then we take a quick tour of Lectora exploring the screen, the ribbons, the different modes, and getting help. We also explore how it stores its files on your computer.
Have It Your Way	Now that you know a little bit about Lectora, learn how to customize the interface to your liking.
Use Other Resources	Okay, you are just starting out and you may want to know where you can learn more or get some help getting those courses out the door. Check out this topic.

Do a Reality Check

This book is for people who are new to Lectora and want to learn quickly how to develop (not *design*) e-learning (computer based training) courses using Lectora. It takes you step-by-step through creating a course. It gives you tips and "best practices" on what works well and what does not. It uses the 80/20 rule – it covers what you use 80% of the time. The other 20% is in my other books or Lectora Help.

Goal of This Book

It is not an application "bible" or handbook. It is not a rehash of the user guide. We could just go through the functions of all the menus and buttons, what they do, and how they work. How exciting would that be? Trivantis provides an excellent Help in the application and a 400+ page Help PDF. Why repeat that?

Instead, this book steps you through the process of how to build a course from the ground up. As you do that, you learn some valuable design tips, best practices, and things to watch out for. When you finish this book, you should be able to use Lectora well enough to develop a basic online training (e-learning) course. In this book you will learn how to:

- Create a Lectora Title

- Create navigation to allow the learner to move through the course

- Add Chapters, Sections, and Pages
- Add text, pictures, graphics, sound, and movies
- Create pop-up windows which display additional information at key points
- Create engaging exercises where the learner applies what he/she is learning
- Create tests and surveys
- Publish this course so you can run it from a network server or from a Learning Management System (LMS)

What This Book Does *Not* Cover

Windows® vs. Mac	This book is written for Windows® users. If you are a Mac user, file locations and how you work in the operating system may be slightly different.
Desktop vs. Online version	This book is for the *desktop* version Lectora 11, not the online version. There are significant differences between the two.
Intermediate and advanced techniques	This book *introduces* you to the basic uses of actions, groups, and variables and shows you how to use them for the most common tasks. The follow-on book, *Lectora 301: Techniques for Professionals*, covers these topics in depth along with most any topic you do not find covered in this book like forms, closed captioning, etc..
All the details	It does not cover every detail about each item or function. Lectora Help does that.
E-learning design	This book is about how to use Lectora but that will *not* guarantee that you create a good e-learning course. As great as it is, Lectora is just a tool. When someone goes to a hardware store to buy a drill bit, they really don't want a drill bit, they want a *hole*. The drill bit is only a means to an end. Just because you can use MS Word® does not mean you can write a good book. So it is with Lectora. It is a tool to help you train people, not an end in itself. About 75% of the effort is in the instructional *design*, not in the development in Lectora. If you do not have formal training in *e-learning* design, get the book, *Designing Effective eLearning: A Step-by-Step Guide* from the same place you got this book.

Inspire tools	This course covers Lectora but *not* any of the tools that come with Lectora Inspire including ReviewLink, Camtasia, Flypaper, SnagIt!
Graphic layout	Nor does this book teach you how to do the basics of graphic layout such as how to create and format text, click and drag, resize an object on the screen. See the Prerequisites next.

Prerequisites

This book is about Lectora, not about basic computer skills.

- You should be familiar with how Microsoft® Office 2007 or 2010 uses ribbons instead of toolbars. This a major change in Lectora 11 from previous versions.

- You should be comfortable with performing the basics functions in a tool such as PowerPoint® where you create text blocks, move and resize them, change font color, size, and face, add shapes, move and align shapes and text blocks. This book will show you how to do the same things in Lectora but it will expect that you know how to do these things in some other tool.

- You should have Lectora installed and know how to launch it.

- Either you should know how to use a drawing tool like PhotoShop®, Corel Draw®, Fire-Works®, PowerPoint®, etc. or know someone who can because most e-learning requires some graphics.

What Is Lectora Anyway?

Lectora is a computer application primarily designed to help trainers develop web-based training (e-learning, CBT). It allows you, the developer, to assemble a wide variety of information in the form of text, pictures, graphics, audio, video, animation, and other files like PDFs to create an e-learning course that can be standalone or viewed using an internet browser.

Lectora comes in three versions:

- Lectora Publisher for the desktop (covered in this book)

- Lectora Inspire for the desktop, which is Lectora Publisher plus some additional integrated tools including Camtasia, FlyPaper, and SnagIt.

- Lectora Online which uses a browser interface and allows multiple people in distributed locations to work on the same course at the same time (Note that there are significant differences between the desktop version and the online version.)

While Lectora does have drawing capabilities, they are not extensive. Its abilities are limited compared to PhotoShop® or even PowerPoint®. Generally, people develop more complicated graphics in other applications and import them into Lectora.

While it does have some limited audio and video editing, these editors are there primarily to enable you to synchronize things that happen on the screen with the audio or video.

Lectora is designed to create e-learning courses for the web and for mobile learning. It can also be used to build websites (I did) although it does have several limitations some of which you can get around using HTML embedded in Lectora.

How Does Lectora Compare to PowerPoint®?

There are some similarities to PowerPoint® and some differences. Here is a list of the biggest ones for those new to Lectora but already familiar with PowerPoint® 2007 or 2010.

Similarities

They both:

- Use the Microsoft® Office ribbon interface approach.
- Can add items to the Quick Access Toolbar and create keyboard shortcuts.
- Open dialog or options windows to access additional characteristics/options for item on the screen.
- Take similar approaches to formatting text and use similar icons.
- Take similar approaches to positioning and sizing shapes and text blocks on the page.
- Allow you to drag and drop items onto a page.
- Use common keyboard shortcuts like Ctrl+X for cut, Ctrl+C for copy, Ctrl+V for Paste, and Ctrl+Z for undo.
- Show things that are not physically on the page. PowerPoint® uses the Master pages for background items and Lectora uses something called "inheritance."
- Use the right-click menu to quickly access common functions.
- Provide guides for you to aid in aligning items on the screen.
- Use the Page Up and Page Down keys to move from one page to the next.
- Allow you to group objects.

Differences

PowerPoint®	Lectora 11
Includes an extensive drawing engine with extensive shape formatting, shapes, predefined objects (SmartArt), and graphic effects (crop, shadow, fade, transparency, contrast, brightness, rotate, etc.).	Uses a limited set of graphic objects and graphic formatting. Lectora did not intend to replace existing drawing applications. Most people develop their graphics using other tools like PhotoShop®, Corel Draw®, Illustrator®, or PowerPoint®. Then they import them using one of a variety of ways.
Has a wide variety of animations that can be applied to most any object.	Has a limited number "animations" that work *only* as an object appears or disappears from the screen. Lectora refers to these as "transitions."
Can add items to ribbons in 2010 as well as to the Quick Access Toolbar.	Can only add items to the Quick Access Toolbar, not the ribbons.
Has limited things that can happen when an object is moused over or clicked.	Has a wide range of possible actions that can happen when an object is moused over or clicked.
Cannot keep track of things that have or have not been done.	Can keep track of things which enable the developer to have different things show as needed (like checkmarks next to completed items).
Keeps its text and graphics source in a single file. (In reality, it is a zipped file. If you change the file extension from PPTX to ZIP, you can open it and see what is inside.)	Keeps its source in multiple files and folders. See the Lectora File Structure topic later in this chapter. This also means that you *cannot* launch a Lectora Title from a zipped file like you can PowerPoint®. You *must unzip* the file first into a regular folder.
Produces output that is *not* directed at the internet but is usually a single file that someone views. For larger files with audio and video, this can be a problem when viewed over a network.	Primarily produces output to some form of HTML so it can be easily viewed over a network using a web browser. It can also produce a single file containing the entire course for viewing.
Produces output that is *not* friendly to Learning Management Systems which track student registration, attempts, completions, and scores.	Can easily produce output that communicates with Learning Management Systems.
Has no built in capability to ask the student questions and give feedback.	Has extensive built in set of question types, testing, and survey capabilities.
Does *not* change the save icon 🖫 after saving the file.	Changes the save icon from 🖫 to 🖫 after saving.

PowerPoint®	**Lectora 11**
Does *not* have alignment tools *readily* available unless you customize a ribbon. You have to click some dropdown list or use the right click menu and select it from there.	Has the alignment tools always readily available at the bottom of the Lectora window. 
Can change the colors in the color selection panel.	Cannot change the colors in the color selection panel. You can save about 16 colors in the **Custom** option. 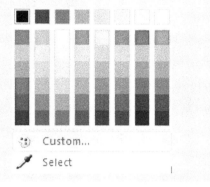
Drawing shapes can contain text.	Shapes are only shapes. Text must be put in a separate text block and positioned on top of the shape.
Does *not* make the selection pane easily available and when it is, you can only hide and show objects.	Has the selection pane always readily available in the form of the **Title Explorer** on the left side of course window. In it you can drag things from one page to another or change which is in front by simply dragging them around.
Accesses resources like graphics, audio, and video either by browsing or using drag and drop from another Windows® folder.	Makes common resource libraries readily available using tabs on the right side of the Lectora window.
Limits the Page Up and Page Down keys to just moving between pages.	Extends the Page Up and Page Down keys beyond moving between pages to viewing what is comparable to PowerPoint® "master" pages. If you encounter a Section "master" so you can see exactly what is there that is common to all the pages in the Section. It does the same for a Chapter.
Groups of objects can contain groups.	Groups of objects cannot contain groups.

Explore the Lectora Interface

As we explore Lectora, it would be great if you opened Lectora and looked around yourself. Try a few things out. See what else it there.

What's on the Screen

On the below is the basic Lectora screen. If you are using Microsoft® Office 2007 or 2010, some of this should already look familiar.

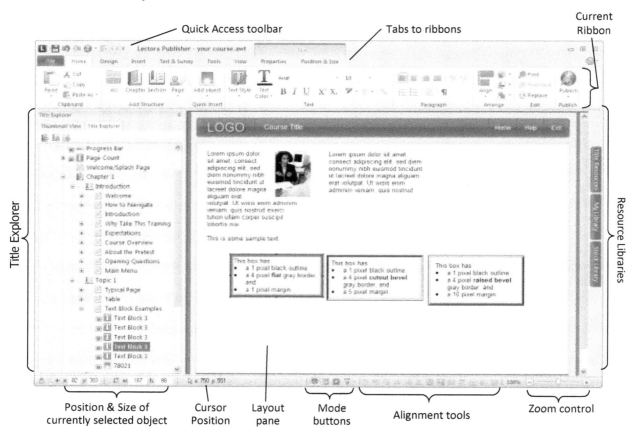

- Across the top you will see the Quick Access Toolbar. It is customizable just like the ones in MS Office. You can add icons (buttons) for things you do frequently.

- Below that are the tabs that get you to the various ribbons. These are similar to those in MS Office applications. Each ribbon is composed of groups of icons (buttons) that perform various functions.

  You can press Ctrl+F1 to collapse the ribbon if you need the space. You can press Ctrl+F1 again to expand it.

Warning 1: If your Lectora window is not wide enough, many of the ribbons will *not* look like what you see in this book. Different ribbons need different amounts of space. You should expand the window as wide as it will go and then close it back up until just before groups start compressing.

- Down the left is the Title Explorer. It shows a list of the Chapters, Sections, Pages, and the objects on the pages in outline form. You can drag and drop things around there as needed. When you click on a page or an object on a page, the page appears to the right in the layout area.

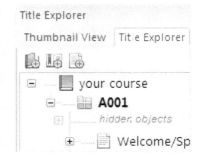

- Down the right side are three tabs that allow you to access easily your resource libraries.

- In the middle is the page layout area, sometimes called the layout pane or the WYSIWYG ("what you see is what you get") interface. Here you arrange the objects on the page like text blocks, pictures, images, etc. and enter text.

- Across the bottom are:

    - The position and size of the current object. You can change these for very precise positioning or sizing on the screen.

    - The current cursor position

    - The mode buttons which allow you to easily switch from Edit to other modes such as Run, Preview, and Preview in Browser

    - Alignment and sizing tools

    - The zoom control

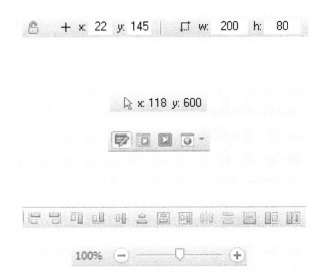

Ribbons

Let's take a brief look at the ribbons. We will cover the tools on each one as we need them to create your course. Some ribbons are always present like the File, Home, Design, Insert, Test & Survey, Tools and View ribbons. Other ribbons like Properties, Position & Size, and others appear depending on what is currently selected.

File Ribbon

The File ribbon is not actually a ribbon. It looks and acts much like the File tab in MS Office MS Word® or PowerPoint®. Here you can save the current Title, open a Title, close the current Title, etc.

The Title Information tab gives the usual information about the file. It also allows you to Enable Author Control and enter a password. Then any object can be protected by clicking the

Author Control icon in the first group on the Properties ribbon.

Save Options

The **Save** options gives you the usual selections. I personally do *not* use **Save As** or **Save A Copy** because it is easy to misplace your files. Instead, go into the operating system (Windows® Explorer) and copy the entire folder. Then to launch the copy, first change its file name to be unique. Then double click on it to open Lectora.

You can also save your course as a **Template**. Then you can use it later to create a new course. I usually just copy an old course and strip out what I don't need. You can waste a lot of time perfecting a template.

Create New Title

In the **Create New Title** tab, you have many options to give you a jump start or ideas on creating new **Titles**. Because most course requirements are unique, a good way to use these is to just create the **Title** and look it over for ideas, then build your own.

Import

In the **Import** tab, you have several selections that allow you to import Lectora content from PowerPoint®, Lectora Online, XML, and a previously zipped Lectora **Title**. The PowerPoint® option is also available in the Import group on the **Tools** ribbon. It is discussed at length in Importing Pages from PowerPoint® on page 194.

Export

The **Export** tab gives you the ability to export your content to MS Word®, Lectora Online, XML, or a ZIP file. The export to MS Word® includes *only* text.

Print

When you click on the **Print** option, it opens a **Print** dialog window where you elect to print your pages in a variety of layouts.

Lectora Preferences

When you click on the **Lectora Preferences**, it opens a **Preferences** dialog window with many of its own tabs. We go over the main ones later in this chapter on page 19.

Home Ribbon

The Home ribbon provides most of the usual functions allowing you to cut, copy, paste, add the more common items like **Chapters** and **Pages**, as well as format and layer text.

Design Ribbon

The Design ribbon lets you set the characteristics (properties) of the entire course much like the Design ribbon does in PowerPoint®. You can select from multiple themes, use a background wizard, set the background properties like color and image, the default text style for text in your course and how one page transitions into another.

Insert Ribbon

The Insert ribbon gives you an easy way to insert all kinds of things into your course. (These things are referred to as "objects" in Lectora speak.)

Test & Survey Ribbon

The Test & Survey ribbon lets you add tests, surveys, questions, and forms into your course. You can also customize how radio buttons and check boxes look. If you are creating a lot of questions, you can create them in a CSV file and import them using this ribbon.

Tools Ribbon

The Tools ribbon gives you tools to create and edit audio and video. You can find where specific variables and images are used in your course. There is a tool to aid with translation from one language to another. (See the appendix on Translation in this book.) This ribbon gives you access to Spell Check and Notes to document your course along with some tools to help when it comes time to have your course reviewed by others.

View Ribbon

The View ribbon lets you see how your course will look and behave from the learner's perspective. It also gives you access to tools that help with layout like the Grid, Guides, and Zoom.

Properties Ribbon

Properties are characteristics or attributes of an item (object) in your course. Most properties are options that you can set. Some of the common properties are:

- the object's name
- whether or not it is locked for author control
- its background color and border
- whether or not it shows when the page shows (is it initially hidden?)
- how an object transitions into view and how it transitions out of view
- a brief description of the object

The Properties ribbon changes depending on the currently selected item (object) to show the properties that belong to that object.

You can click on the lower right corner of the leftmost group on the Properties ribbon to open a window where you can enter a brief description of the object. This is very useful when you are describing some complex actions in your course or perhaps a text block that has changing contents.

You can click on the lower right corner of the Appearance group to specify the CSS style sheet to be used to change the appearance of this object.

Appearance

Speed Tip 1: Probably the fastest way to switch to the Properties ribbon is by double clicking on the object's icon in the Title Explorer or by double clicking on any object except a text block in the layout pane. (When you double click on a text block, your mouse arrow turns to an I-beam so you can enter text.)

Position & Size Ribbon

The Position & Size ribbon lets you lock the object to prevent it from being accidently moved, see and change position and size of the object, and reset it to its original size.

Action Ribbon

The Action ribbon lets you add and change actions. We discuss actions in Step 5: Make Things Happen on page 107.

Dialog Windows

Some objects like questions and menus have more properties/options than can conveniently be displayed on the Properties ribbon. When this happens, Lectora opens a dialog window (sometimes called a dialog box, wizard, or creator) to display all the options and allow you to change them.

Here is an example of the Question Creator dialog window. Notice that there are three tabs to allow you to control the question, the feedback, and the number of attempts.

Modes

Lectora has five modes of operation.

Edit mode	In Edit mode you develop your courses. Here you add, change, delete, format, arrange, etc. things.
Run mode	In Run mode you see how your course looks and acts when the learner is using it. You still the ribbons, Title Explorer, etc. although all editing functions are disabled.
Preview mode	Preview mode is similar to Run mode except that the entire window is covered and all you can see is your course running.
Preview in Browser	This opens a new window and shows only the current page in a browser. Sometimes there are differences between Edit/Run/Preview modes and how things look and behave in a browser. You press the Escape key to exit this mode and return to Edit mode.
Debug mode	This mode is a variation of Run mode except that a second window opens up to show you the details of how things are behaving behind the scenes. It is available on the View ribbon.

Getting Help

The makers of Lectora have provided a wealth of help with this version of Lectora.

You can click on the question mark icon in the upper right corner of the Lectora window.

On many ribbons, you will this icon on the right. Click it for detailed information on the tools on that ribbon.

Some tools open a dialog window. In the bottom right of the window you will see a Help button. You can click it to get help on that dialog window.

The video editor and the audio editor have their own Help available when the editors are open.

If you don't see a Help button, just press the F1 key.

While this built-in help is nice and handy, sometimes I have had trouble finding what I want. I have had better luck searching the User Guide PDF. One is installed when you installed Lectora but it may not be current. You can go to the folder where Lectora was installed and create a shortcut to it. For Lectora Professional on Windows® XP, the file is located here.

"C:\Program Files\Trivantis\Lectora Publisher\Docs\Lectora_User_Guide.pdf"

You can go to www.Lectora.com > Support and find the current PDF.

In addition to the Help built into Lectora, you can also go to www.Lectora.com and click on Lectora U. There you will find a wealth of information on how to do things in Lectora. Here is what it looked like when this book was written.

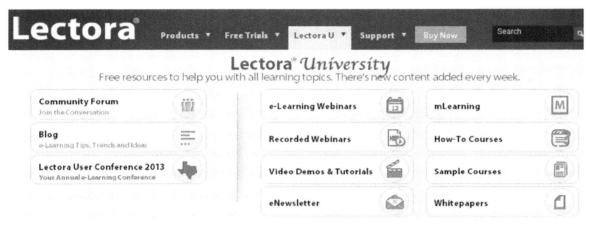

Still More Help

Contact the author, Benjamin Pitman, ben.pitman@eProficiency.com or 678-571-4179.

Get to Know the Lectora File Structure

Unlike many other applications like MS Word® or PowerPoint®, Lectora does *not* store all of its information in a single file. There are multiple files and folders for a single course (Title). Here is what it looks like in Windows® XP.

If you have added additional files such as PDFs, there will be an additional folder called "extern" for them.

When you publish to the Web (HTML) the published files are in this folder. You do not need to navigate to here to launch your course. You can do it from by clicking the Preview button on the Publish window.

The images folder contains all the graphics used in your course.

If your course contains audio or video files, there will be a media folder that holds them.

If you published to SCORM, the output will be here.

The file beginning with ~$ is the auto-save information. This is the recovery information that preserves your recent work. Just open your course and reply Yes to get these updates applied.

The .awt file is the main file for your course. It does *not* contain any graphics, or audio/video files. **To work on your course, just double click this file.**

The .bmp file is simply an image of the last page you worked on.

The .ini file contains is a system file used by Lectora to keep track of where you are and the current expansion of the Title Explorer.

There may be others depending on what you have added to your course.

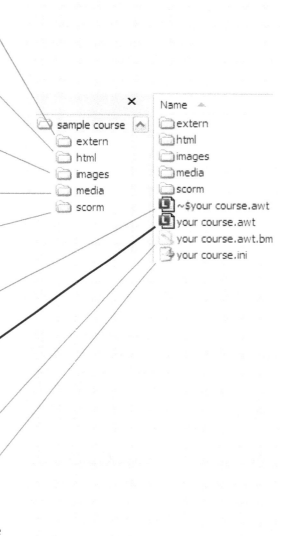

Cne of my personal recommendations is to keep all of your support files that belong to the course ir. the same folder. I add a folder called "graphics, etc." where I put the source of anything that belcngs to the course. It includes:

- my original storyboard along with any review documents,

- a PowerPoint® file there with all my drawings and treated pictures,

- any graphics clients have sent,

- any specially sized ones where I needed to use FireWorks®,

- and pretty much anything that I used to create the course.

If anyone else ever has to work on your course, everything is in one folder, the course folder.

Customize Your Lectora Interface

There are several ways to customize your Lectora interface. Look this section over briefly, so you know what you can do. Then as you get more familiar with Lectora, come back here and apply some of these techniques so you can be more efficient.

Adding Items to the Quick Access Toolbar

If you do something a lot, it may be quicker to add it to the Quick Access Toolbar.

Right click on any ribbon and select Customize Quick Access Toolbar...

In the dialog window that appears, use the dropdown lists to select items to add to the Quick Access Toolbar.

Creating Shortcut Keys

Some commands in Lectora already have built-in shortcut keystrokes that are shown when you mouse over the icon. Here is an example for the Cut command. The shortcut is shown in ( ) next to the command name.

There are two shortcut keys in Edit mode that can be very useful if you are cruising through your course looking for something.

Page Up takes you to the previous page.

Page Down takes you to the next page.

Some people like to set up their own shortcut keys. I use one to add Notes to the pages.

1. Right click on any ribbon and select Customize Quick Access Toolbar…

2. Near the bottom of the dialog window you will see Keyboard shortcuts. Click on the Customize… button and create shortcuts.

3. Select the desired command at the top.

4. After you have entered the new key, be sure to click the Assign button or else it will not take.

Setting Your Preferences

PowerPoint® has Options; Lectora has Preferences. There are several preferences that will make it easier to develop your course or make it look better.

- Click on the File tab and click on Lectora Preferences near the bottom.

- On the General tab, check the Show buttons for hiding objects in the Title Explorer and Show visibility check boxes in Title Explorer.

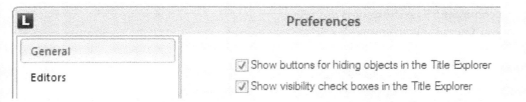

This will allow you to make better use of the Title Explorer by being able to hide the objects you don't want to see right now because they are in front of objects you want to work on.

This  becomes

- The Editors area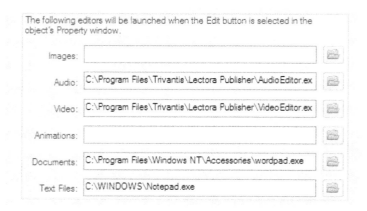

  allows you to specify applications to use to edit your objects. If they are not filled in, click the folder button beside one you want to set and navigate to where the application is. Most are already set for Lectora Inspire.

- Set your Auto Update

  Auto Update

  to 1 day so you get updates as soon as they come out.

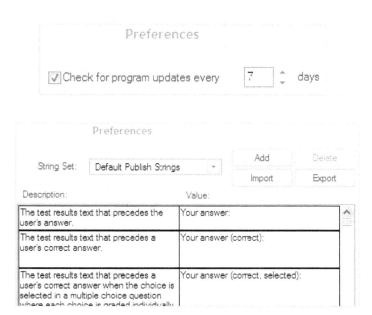

- In the Publish Strings tab,

  Publish Strings

  you can change the default messages that appear in various dialog boxes when the learners use the course. You can also export these if you have the need for different sets as with different clients or languages.

- The Publish Messages tab

  Publish Messages

  allows you to have some control as to which messages appear when you publish your course. Come back to this and make any desired changes after you have used Lectora for a while.

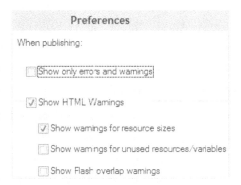

- The Form Elements tab

  Form Elements

  allows you to have much nicer looking buttons and check boxes than the default ones. You can apply different selections to different Titles by clicking the Apply to Current Title button at the bottom. You can also set these on the Test & Survey ribbon.

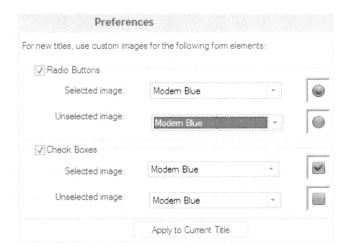

Setting Your Save Options

This is a *very* important.

1. On the File menu, click Save Options.

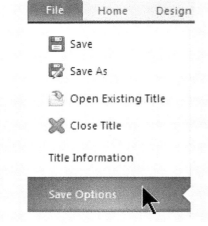

2. At the bottom, check Enable Auto Save and set it to save every 1 minute.

Customizing Your View

In addition to your preferences, there are a few things you should set to control your view. Click on the View ribbon.

1. Some people like Grids but I have found that Guides seem to work better in the end. Guides work as they do in PowerPoint®. They provide an easy way to align objects consistently throughout your course. Begin by clicking Show Rulers.

2. When the rulers appear, click in one. Your cursor will turn to ✛║✛. Drag it onto the course layout to where you want things to line up. A

bright blue line will appear. When you drag objects near it, they will snap-to the guide. You can move the guide by holding down the Ctrl key as you mouse over the guide. It will turn to +‖+ and then you can click and drag the guide to where you want.

3. Another change happened when you created the guide. The Show Guides button is now highlighted. You can click on it to toggle the visibility of the guides. You can also use the keyboard shortcut Ctrl+E.

4. Now the default bright blue color of the guides is a bit annoying to some. To change this, click

on Options button and select a gray color in the dialog box that appears.

Sometimes the layout area gets a little mixed up, especially when you have been working on some things that were behind some others. You can put it all back the way it will be viewed by a learner by either pressing F5 or clicking the Refresh icon in the Display group.

Most people don't, but you can "tear off" the Title Explorer and move it to the side as shown on the left below. To put it back, just click Reset Layout in the Panes group on the View ribbon.

Other Resources

This book covers the fundamentals of creating an e-learning course using Lectora. There are other books and online resources that you can use.

Learn More about *Development* in Lectora:

• *Lectora 201: What They Don't Teach You in Class* by Benjamin Pitman	
• *Lectora 301: Techniques for Professionals* by Benjamin Pitman	
• Other Lectora books can be found by searching the same place you found this book.	
• Free tutorials, tips, toolkit, and other free things to read and expand Lectora	www.eProficiency.com/webStore/ www.quizzicle.com www.artisanelearning.com
• Add-ons and techniques for some price	www.eProficiency.com/webStore/ www.quizzicle.com
• Free webinars, demos, tutorials, how-to courses, sample courses, and white papers	www.Lectora.com > LectoraU
• Training and product user guides	www.Lectora.com > Support

Learn More about *Designing* E-Learning

• *Designing Effective e-Learning: A Step-by-Step Guide*	Search the online bookstores.
• *Superb eLearning using Low-Cost Scenarios: A Step-by-Step Guide to eLearning by Doing* (for any tool)	Search the online bookstores.
• Recommended books	www.eProficiency.com > Recommended Books
• Free tutorials	www.eProficiency.com/webStore/ and click on Instr. Design category

Get Help Designing and Developing Courses

These developers all have a solid knowledge of designing courses for e-learning and development in Lectora:

- Benjamin Pitman (Dr. Lectora) for free advice as well as paid services at www.eProficiency.com

- Jay Lambert at www.integratedlearnings.com

- Diane Elkins at www.artisanelearning.com

- Peter Sorenson at www.quizzicle.com

- Ron Wincek at www.interactiveadvantage.com

Practice What You Learned

Before going on, take some time to explore the various ribbons, especially the File ribbon to be sure you are familiar with what they look like and what is available.

Familiarize yourself with the Lectora file structure as soon as you create your first course shell in the next step.

Remember These Key Points

There are many ways to customize your Lectora interface. As you use Lectora more and more, you will likely want to make further customizations. Remember that you can set these preferences at any time.

- Be sure you have the prerequisites before starting this book.

- Be aware of the differences between Lectora and PowerPoint®.

- The different modes allow you to edit your course content and then see how it will look and act for the learners.

- Customize your Lectora interface using the Quick Access Toolbar, shortcut keys, Preferences, and View.

Step 2: Create Your Course Shell

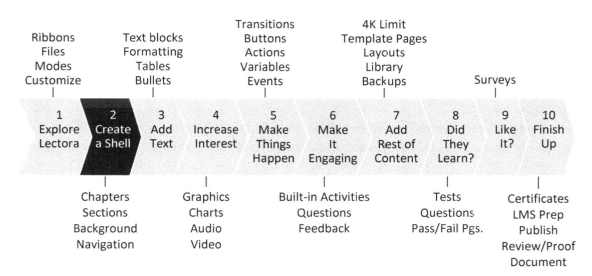

Just a note before we get started. If you want the Lectora Title that I used to create this book with **working examples**, go to www.eProficiency.com/101.html.

Before you can add all the stuff your boss or sponsor wants to the course, you need a course shell. A shell consists of a framework for the course including a couple of blank pages, background images, navigation buttons, and everything else you would see on a blank page.

Here's what we have to do to create your course shell.

Create a Title	First, we open Lectora and step through creating a new Title.
Set the Overall Design	Next, we set some overall design characteristics which set the look of the course.
Add Background Graphics	Most likely, you will need to add some background graphics like a banner and a logo.
Create a Course Structure	After you have the graphics in for a typical page, create the structure of your course that resembles your outline. You do have an outline, don't you?
Add Navigation	No course is complete without some way to move around. Add your navigation buttons and menus next.
Add Progress Indicators	Learners always want to know "Where am I?" This is how you let them know with page numbers and progress bars.
Save for Later	There are a couple of things you need to know about saving courses and they are covered in this step.

Begin by Creating a New Title

"Title" is the term Lectora uses to refer to a course. Lectora offers many templates. You should experiment with these to see what they look like. I have never found them very satisfactory for a given project and always ended up creating one from scratch. However, they do have some very good ideas and are worth exploring. Here's what to do to create a blank course.

1. Launch Lectora.

2. Click New Blank Title.

3. Select Save As from the File ribbon.

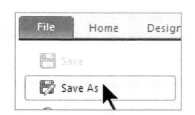

4. In the Save As dialog box that opens, specify the file name and the folder where you want the file to be saved.

5. Click OK.

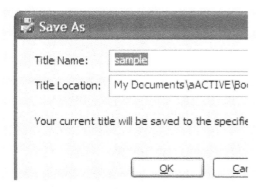

Set the Title Design Characteristics

You can see and change the characteristics (properties) that apply to your entire course on the Design ribbon.

1. Begin by clicking on the Title Options. This will bring up a Title Options dialog window.

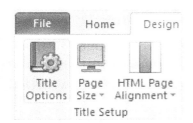

Here you can set an option that supports your course being run from a Learning Management System (LMS). There are other things you need to do besides this and we cover all these in Get Ready for Your LMS If You Use on page 232.

The **Enable Dynamic Text Option** allows you to use text blocks that can be changed *after* your course is published. This can be useful if you have a course that requires different text say for different divisions or different countries. You create and publish your course, put several copies in different locations on your network. Then you can change these text blocks without having to several different source versions of your course.

Check the **Use Web Accessibility Settings** if you are required to make your course compliant to government regulation 508. Click the Help button on this window for more details.

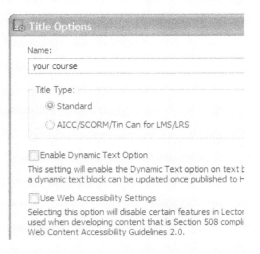

2. Click on the Page Size icon and select your page size from one in the list or set your own. Note that if you have a background image, it should be *exactly* the size you have specified.

Best Practice 1: When picking your page size, consider that the ideal ratio for the body of the screen where most of your content will be displayed is 8 to 5. Use an easy drawing tool like PowerPoint® to draw a rough page layout. When you are finished, create a simple rectangle and cover the area where your course content will be. This does not include the navigation and major heading areas. The ratio of its width to height should be 8 to 5 or about 1.6. Then recreate something close to that in Lectora.

3. Most courses will look better if you select Centered in the HTML Page Alignment property. It won't matter if your LMS sets the window size, but if it does not, then this will look more professional. Note that this only centers the course *horizontally* in the window. If you want it centered both horizontally *and* vertically, check out a free extension from www.quizzicle.com.

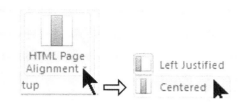

4. If you don't have a background, try some of the Title Themes. If you do, click on Image in the Title Background group and navigate to where you have your background image.

 Best Practice 2: Use a *white* background behind your text and main body area. This will avoid many issues later like these where white is showing where it be transparent.

5. Set your default text style for the page. You can either select a style from the dropdown list or set your own color, font, size, and style. We will discuss Text Styles in depth in the next chapter.

6. If you are concerned with pages flashing as the learner goes from one to the next, click the Page Transitions icon and select a page transition. Wipe Right is a good choice.

   Note: You should try this over your network before you go too far to be sure that it works properly.

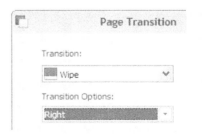

Add Course-wide Graphics

Instead of specifying the background on the Design ribbon, you can add the graphics that will show on every page. Later when we talk more in detail about graphics, you will learn how to add your own in Creating a Custom Background on page 82. For now, click the Design tab and then one of the Title Themes. This will create some standard graphics and buttons and insert them at the Title level. You should now have something like the below.

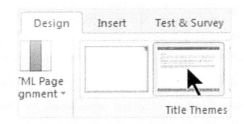

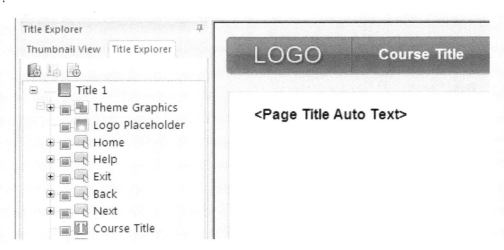

Create an Effective Course Structure

Lectora uses a book metaphor in the Title Explorer. Like a book, a Title can have pages outside chapters and inside chapters. Chapters can have pages and some of those pages can be grouped into sections. Sections can be further subdivided into sub-sections.

Best Practice 3: A good e-learning course does not overwhelm the learner with information. It is about the size of a chapter in a textbook – something like 20-60 pages. This includes overviews, exercises, and summaries.

Best Practice 4: Since page numbering and other progress indicators are Title, Chapter, or Section dependent, a good design is to create one Chapter for your content and then break it down into sections by topic. Use other Chapters for a test, test results, popup pages, and development only pages.

To create the structure of your course:

1. Rename the course from "Title 1" to the name you want your course to have. This is *internal* to your course and does not affect the file name.

2. Rename the default page in your Title to the Welcome or Splash page. This page will be the first page the learner sees when they open the course – much like the cover of a book.

   Some courses use an animation or video on this page. This is a good opportunity to grab the learner's attention. If the information is not essential, allow the learner to skip it.

3. Add a Chapter by either

   – clicking on the Chapter icon in the Add Structure group on the Home ribbon or

   – by clicking on the Add Chapter icon in the Title Explorer.

   This will insert a Chapter and one blank page into your course.

4. At this point, I recommend you delete this Page and add Sections that correspond to the topics in your course. Click on Chapter 1 in the Title Explorer.

5. Then click the Add Section icon. This will add one Section and a blank page to the Chapter.

6. To add additional Sections, repeat this, clicking on the Chapter icon *each time before* adding a Section.

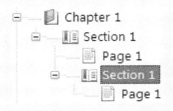

 Warning 2: You must click on the Chapter in the Title Explorer before adding each Section, otherwise the Sections will be embedded within the first Section and become a sub-section like you see here.

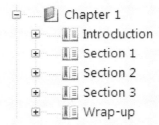

• Then rename them for the course topics. Here is a good solid e-learning course structure.

Add Your Navigation

Generally speaking there are three kinds of "navigation" you can use in a course.

• Buttons

• Menus

- Tables of Contents

Let's look at how you might use each. You need to consider them now because it affects how you lay out your pages. You don't want to get to the end of a 50 page course and then decide you need to move everything a little to the right or a little down to make room for these things.

Using Buttons

If you used one of the themes, the main navigation buttons, Home, Help, Exit, Back, and Next buttons are already created for you. If you don't like them, you can replace them with ones of your choice. We will cover how to make your own buttons in Use Buttons and Actions to Navigate Around the Course on page 114.

It is a good idea to lock any objects that will appear on all the pages like the background graphics and navigation buttons. You don't want to accidently move them when you are working on a page. Click on the object and then click on the Lock icon in the lower left of the Lectora window. It will change to show the object is locked.

Using Menus

Lectora has a Menu object that allows you to create horizontal or vertical menus with submenus if you need them. The two main uses of menus are:

- to navigate to the different Sections of your course and

- to provide access to additional information.

Navigation Menus

Navigation menus take learners to main parts of the course. They typically go down the left side of the page or across the top.

On the Insert ribbon, click on Menu. This opens the Menu Creator (wizard).

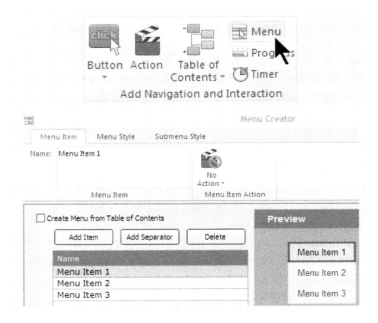

You can easily create a simple menu for course navigation by checking the Create Menu from Table of Contents. Then click the boxes next to any Chapter or Section you do *not* want to appear in your menu.

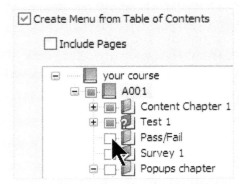

Additional Information Menus

To create a menu that shows additional information, instead of checking the Create Menu from Table of Contents box, you click on a menu item and enter the desired text.

As you name each menu item, you set what you want to happen in the Menu Item Action area.

If you want to have submenus, you click on an item and then click the green indent arrow.

This

becomes this

Now you only have three items at the top level instead of four. When you move your mouse over Documents, it how has a submenu. You can go several levels deep but best practice is to keep it simple.

After you have created a menu, you can open the Menu Creator again by clicking on its icon on the Properties ribbon for the Menu.

You can change many options for the Menu Style and Submenu Style from either inside the Menu Creator or from the additional ribbons that appear when a Menu object is selected. Experiment with them to see what looks best in your course. Note that some, like Windows® 3D Style look a little different when seen through a browser.

Using a Table of Contents

Another way to navigate is to use a Table of Contents (TOC). It is similar to a Menu that uses the TOC but has three different formats.

1. Click Table of Contents on the Insert ribbon.

   This creates a Tree View TOC. When you click on the ⊞ signs, it expands that part of the view (when the course is running) much like it does when you are navigating folders in Windows®.

2. You can change the type of TOC by clicking on Type in the Layout group of the Properties ribbon.

3. You can control what is shown in the Table of Contents by checking the boxes next to the Chapters, Sections, and Pages.

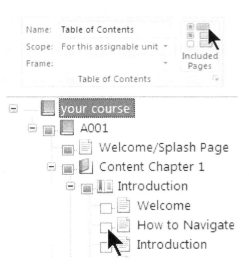

Add Progress Indicators

Progress indicators give learners an idea of where they are in the course. Learners can estimate how much more time they will need to allow. The indicators give learners some sense of accomplishment by showing where they are in the course.

The two most common ways to indicate progress are:

- Page numbers
- A progress bar

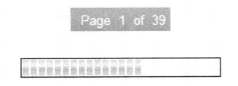

Page numbers are very helpful during the testing and review cycles before your course goes live. They are also useful when learners need to report a problem with a page in the course.

You can also show checkmarks next to a Menu but that is an advanced topic because there is currently no easy way to do that.

Adding Page Numbers to the Chapter

1. Click on the Chapter icon in the Title Explorer. This ensures that the page numbers will appear on *all* the Pages in the Chapter, not just the last one you were working on.

2. Click on **Page Number** on the **Insert** ribbon.

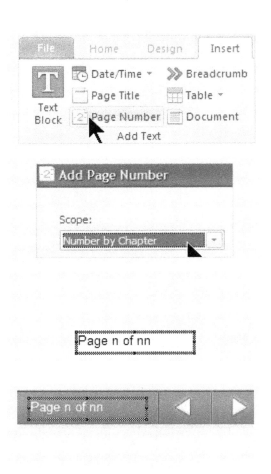

3. In the dialog window, select **Number by Chapter** in the **Scope** dropdown box.

4. Set the font and text style and click **OK**. This will create a text block in the upper left corner of the course window that is filled with the page number when the course actually is running. In **Edit** mode, it will just show "Page n of nn".

5. Click on the text block and drag it to where you want it. A good choice is somewhere near the navigation buttons. You may need to change the text font, size, and color the same way you would for any other text block.

Adding a Progress Bar

1. On the **Insert** ribbon, click on **Progress Bar** in the **Add Navigation** group.

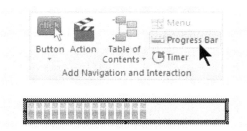

A standard green progress bar will appear.

2. Click on its Properties ribbon and select Table of Contents from the Custom dropdown list.

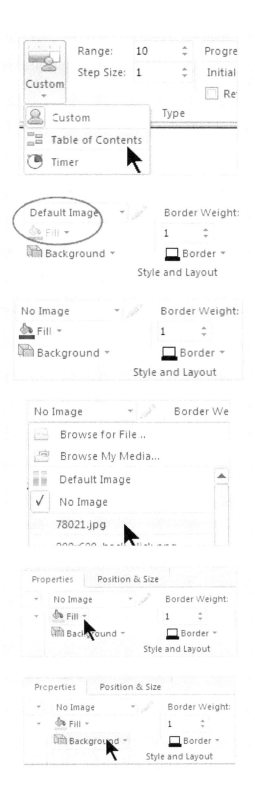

The image selection dropdown list and the Fill specify what is to slide across the bar to show progress.

Specify how you want your Progress Bar to indicate progress.

- If you select No Image, then you can select a Fill color to fill the bar as you progress from the options in the Style and Layout group.

- If you want to use a custom image that moves across the bar as you progress, navigate to it using the Default Image dropdown box in the Style and Layout group.

- If you just want a color,
  - select No Image and
  - then select the desired Fill color.

3. Select the desired Border Weight and Border color.

4. If you want a background color other than white, use the Background property to change it.

5. Resize and position your progress bar.

Ir Edit mode, it will look partially full as shown here.

Once your course is running it will progress across the bar.

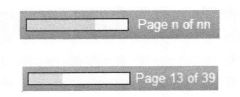

Working with Inheritance

In Lectora, not all objects that *appear* on a page are actually *on* that page. It would be very laborious to have to manually put the navigation buttons on each and every page. If you wanted to reposition them, you would have to go to every page and move them. That would be too much work.

PowerPoint® uses Master pages which allows you to create the background to slides in one place. Lectora uses something similar to the Master pages called Inheritance. Inheritance allows you to put objects like the navigation buttons, logos, background graphics at a higher level such as the Title or Chapter level and they are "inherited" by all the "children" (Chapters, Sections, Pages) under them. If you put an object on a Chapter, it is inherited by all the Sections and Pages it contains but not other Chapters. If it is visible like a button or a logo, then you can see it on every Page even though it only occurs once in the Title. If it is an action that does something like set the current page number, then that something runs on every page.

In the example to the right,

- The blue_header will appear on the Welcome Page, and in all Chapters.

- The chapter heading will appear on all the pages in all Sections in that Chapter but *not* in the next Chapter.

- The Section icon will appear on all the pages in that Section but *not* any other Section in that Chapter or any other Chapter.

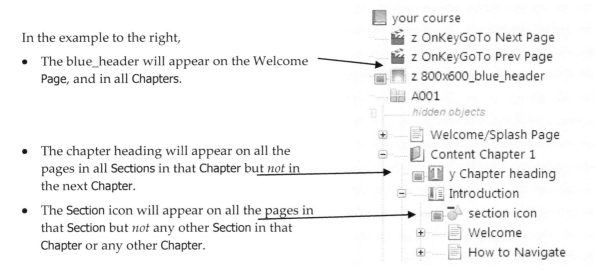

Excluding Objects

There are times when you do not want an object inherited on a Chapter or a Page. For example, does it make sense to have a Back button on the first page or a Next button on the last?

1. To exclude and object from a Page, first click on the Page in the Title Explorer and then on Inherit on its Properties ribbon.

In the Inheritance Settings dialog window:

2. Select Specific objects from parents from the dropdown list.

3. Then click on any object that you want excluded and move them to the Excluded side by clicking on the >>>.

Save Your Course

It is good practice to save your course every few minutes. To save your work you can either:

- click on the Save icon at the top of the Lectora window, or

Once saved, this icon turns gray.

- click on Save on the File ribbon, or

- use the common keystroke combination Ctrl+S.

Best Practice 5: If you want to copy your course, *avoid* using Save As because it is sometimes difficult to find exactly where you saved your course. Instead, in Windows®, copy the folder that contains all these files. Then change its name.

Best Practice 6: Launch your course for editing in Lectora simply by double clicking on the file icon in its Windows® folder. This is faster than launching Lectora and then navigating to the course file. *It is also more reliable* because you know exactly *where* your course is i.e. which version you are working with.

Practice What You Learned

We have covered a lot in this step. Before going on, take some time to create your own course shell and apply these techniques so that the know-how stays with you.

After you have created your course shell, take a look at the file structure in Windows® Explorer.

Remember These Key Points

- Be sure to check the folder where you think you created your new Title using Windows® Explorer to be sure it is actually there.

- If possible, use only one Chapter for the content and divide that Chapter into Sections. If you have a Chapter with more than about 60 pages, you probably should use several Chapters to avoid scaring learners with something like Page 1 of 245. Better yet, break it into several courses.

- Use Menus and Tables of Contents to give learners easy access to various parts of the course.

Step 3: **Add and Format Text**

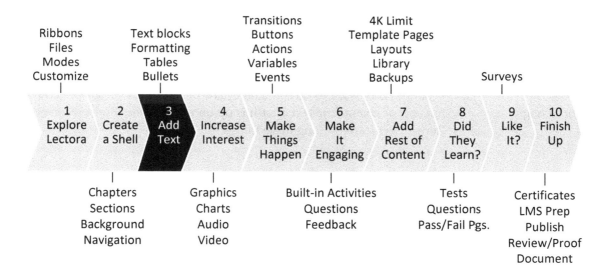

Now that you have your course shell in place, you are ready to add the real meat of most courses, the text. While adding text is fairly easy, there are many options when it comes to doing it right.

To add text to your course:

Clean Up First	The process of creating the shell created a little mess that needs to be cleaned up first.
Set the Page Properties	You can really do this anytime, but might as well get started on the right foot by configuring the page the way you want it. You will need this later.
Insert Text	This is what you have been waiting for, a lot of either typing or copying and pasting. Bet you can't wait.
Format It	It is not enough just to paste that text in; it has to look nice. Here you learn how to format text in Lectora.
Create Special Text Blocks	Most text blocks are just text but sometimes you want to have a background color, margin, and border. This is where you learn how to do that.
Check Your Spelling and Grammar	Lectora can help you with spelling and you can export to MS Word® for the grammar but you have to make the changes manually back in Lectora. If you have a good storyboard, you won't need this.
Apply Good Design	There are an infinite number of ways to lay out a page. Apply these design guidelines to get a learner-friendly text pages.
Not Enough?	You may still want to do some fancy stuff like use CSS, translate your course, or change the text after it is up on your server. Here we cover how to get started doing these things.

Clean Up First

Before we start adding more text blocks, we first need to clean up what we already have.

If you use one of the Title themes, it comes with a preformatted page title shown here. It is filled automatically with the name of the current page using an action (discussed later). The page name is the name on the page in the Title Explorer. While you can reformat this text block, using this technique to create a page title has a several *disadvantages*.

<Page Title Auto Text>

- It is generally a good idea to use reasonably short page names in the Title Explorer, because
  - long ones can be difficult to read if you have a table of contents and
  - long page names can cause horizontal scrolling in the Title Explorer.

  For these reasons, you may want the page title and the page name to be different.

- If you export the course to MS Word®, the pages are not labeled in the exported text – that is, they will not have a title on them.

- If you print your course to a PDF, the pages will not be labeled.

- And most important, *spell check does not check the names* in the Title Explorer because many people use abbreviations.

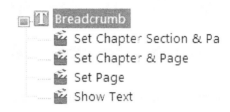

So, let's start by deleting the Page Title text block that now shows up on every page. Click on it anywhere and delete it using Ctrl+X, the Delete key, or any other method you choose.

Set the Page Properties

Once you have a page added, you can set its properties, which are generally the same as the ones you see on the Design ribbon that apply to the entire course. You can make the page a different size, align differently, exclude some objects that would normally appear on the page like buttons, etc., change its background color or image, use a different text style, or even have a different transition. This last one is a nice touch for the first page of each topic. For the most part, there is no need to change the page properties except for popup windows, which we discuss later in this book.

If you want to learn more about any of these properties, just click the Help icon at the right end of the ribbon.

Help

If you do not have a test in your course, on the last page of the course, somehow disable the Next button. A common way to do that is to Exclude it from being inherited as we described earlier.

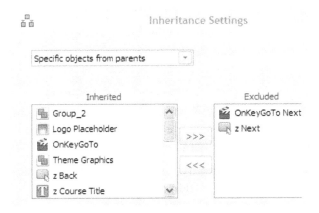

1. On the Properties ribbon for the page, click Inherit.

2. Click on each object that would take you to the next page and click the arrows to move them to the Excluded column.

Insert Text

Like other drawing tools, text cannot be just typed on the page, you must enter it into a text block. First you have to create the text block and then add the text. The two most common blocks of text on a page are the page title and the page body. Here are the steps to create them.

Creating Text Blocks

1. To insert a text block, click on the large text block icon  on either the Home or Insert ribbon. You will see a text block like this.

2   Insert a second text block and drag away from the first.

3. Resize them as you would any text block in PowerPoint® by clicking on an edge to resize it.

4. Click once on the name in the Title Explorer and change the name of one text block to "Page Title" and the other to "Body." You can make this change in the Name field on the Properties ribbon or by slowly clicking once more on the name in the Title Explorer.

Best Practice 7: Give meaningful names to most your text blocks, not just these. Later on it will help you work with them when you need to change them or create actions that show and hide the text blocks.

5. Now double click on the Page Title text block in the layout pane and enter your title. Click on the Body text block and add some sample text. You can also copy and paste text from other applications.

Sample Page Title

Sample page body text. Lorem consect adipiscing elit, sed dien euismod tincidunt ut lacreet dol erat volutpat. Ut wisis enim adn

Warning 3: Never just copy and paste text from other applications except NotePad **because they embed formatting codes that may not show in Lectora.** When you publish these to so you can view them through a browser, hidden numbering, bullets, etc. may appear.

You should always copy and Paste Unformatted by selecting it from the Paste dropdown list.

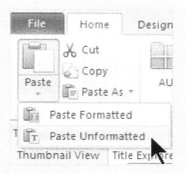

Speed Tip 2: If you are doing a lot of this kind of pasting, either:

- Copy it all from the source document and paste it into a NotePad document which strips out all the formatting. Then copy and paste from there using Ctrl+C and paste using Ctrl+V or

- Modify your Quick Access Toolbar and add the Paste Unformatted icon to it.

- Or use the Ctrl+Shift+V keyboard shortcut. (little finger on Ctrl, ring finger on Shift, index finger on V)

Speed Tip 3: For a variety of reasons, sometimes the text block can end up being smaller than the text requires. This results in missing text when published. You can resize the text block using its sizing handles or you can *simply double click in it* and it will expand downward to the right size.

Format the Text for a Professional Looking Course

Text in Lectora like most word processors has two types of formatting:

- Text formatting – bold, italic, color, font face, size, etc.
- Paragraph formatting – paragraph and line spacing, bullets, indent

Formatting Text

The tools to format text shown here are located roughly in the middle of the Home ribbon. You will see them in several other places where you need to apply text formatting like Menus.

When choosing a font, you should consider its readability and availability.

Readability: Serif fonts are used in printed material like this book. They are *not* good for reading on a computer screen due to the much lower resolution of computer screens (96 dots per inch on a screen vs. 300 or more in print). They are harder to read on the computer than sans-serif fonts like Arial or Verdana.

Availability: Not all computers have all fonts. If a computer does not have the font specified, it will substitute another one, which may take more or less space. Here is a list of web-safe *easily readable* generally *available* fonts. Verdana is probably the best choice as it was specifically designed for computer use, Arial second.

For body text, 11-12 point Arial or 10-12 Verdana are probably the best. Some people prefer 14 point. Remember, people are reading this like a book, not a presentation on a big screen with someone talking.

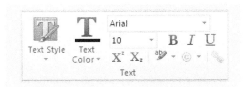

Times Roman, Bookman, etc.

Arial   **Arial black**
Courier New **Impact**
Trebuchet MS Comic Sans MS
Verdana

Sample   Arial 11
Sample   Verdana 10
Sample   Verdana 11
Sample   Arial 12
Sample   Verdana 12

Web 2.0 has led us to using slightly larger font size but *not* bold text for the page title.

Several years ago, you might use 16pt bold Arial font for a heading.

Today we bump up the size a couple of points and use regular style (not bold). This second one seems a bit easier to read and looks a bit more elegant. It is really up to you and your stakeholders.

Dark text on a light background is easier to read and will be remembered better.

Avoid lots of light text on dark background. Save that for titles or emphasis.

You can apply text color using the pallet.

16pt Bold Title

18pt not bold Title

✓ Easy to remember

✗ Harder to remember

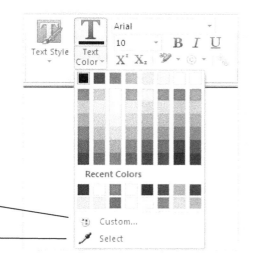

You can specify exact RGB colors by selecting Custom…

Or you can select a color from anywhere on the screen using the eyedropper. More on this later.

Do not use <u>underline</u> for emphasis. Web standard is that underlined text is a hyperlink.

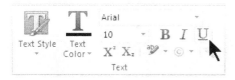

Use **bold** (Ctrl+B) or *italic* (Ctrl+I) for emphasis. Avoid entire paragraphs in bold or italic.

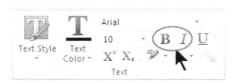

You can use highlighting for emphasis but use it sparingly. Any overused technique will get old and lose it impact.

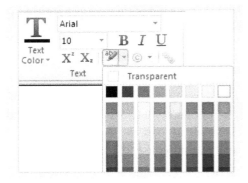

> **Experience may be the best teacher, but it is expensive!**
>
> I saw one course that used several different fonts for the body on different pages and even font sizes. At first, I knew something was different from one page to the next but couldn't figure out what. My focus shifted from the content to the difference. Once I figured it out, I saw it occurring frequently and began to see the course as something less than professionally done.

Best Practice 8: While you can use many different size fonts, font colors, and effects, it is much better to be somewhat conservative. Don't let your course look like a ransom note. ☺

Using Paragraph Formatting

Paragraph formatting tools are located just to the right of the text tools. You can add bullets, adjust paragraph and line spacing, etc. There is nothing special about these tools as most work like similar applications.

You can bulletize your text by selecting some or all of the desired lines and click the bullets icon.

You can also apply bullets using Alt+B keyboard shortcut.

If you want bullets other than the plain round ones, you can use a table, coming up soon.

You can *number* your lines by the desired text and click on the numbering icon to get the below.

1. First point
2. Second point
3. Third point

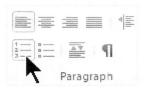

You can change *how* the list is numbered from Arabic numerals to either Roman numerals or letters by

– first clicking on a numbered line

– then right clicking

– then selecting Numbering Options.

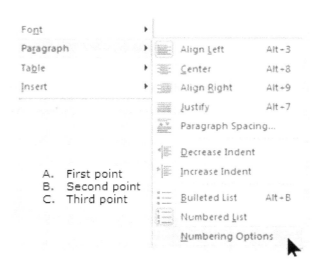

A. First point
B. Second point
C. Third point

There you can also change the starting number in a list. This is useful if you have a numbered list that extends from one text block to another.

You can have several levels of numbered bullets. First create your list and number it.

1. First point
2. Sub point 1
3. Sub point 2
4. Second point
5. Third point

Then select the lines you want at a lower level and click the Increase Indent icon.

1. First point
   a. Sub point 1
   b. Sub point 2
2. Second point
3. Third point

Paragraph spacing may be new to some of you. It allows you to specify the number of points before and after a paragraph as well as spacing between lines.

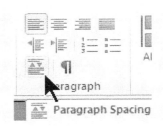

If you are using something like 12 point Verdana font, some good settings are

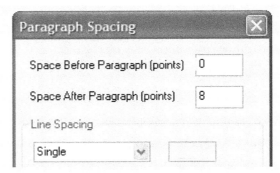

- Single line spacing
- 8 points between each normal paragraph
- 4 points between items in a bulleted or numbered list

Speed Tip 4: How to Quickly Use Adjustable Paragraph Spacing and Line Spacing

Paragraph Spacing and Line Spacing are not yet part of a Lectora Text Style (discussed next) like they are in MS Word® so to implement it you have to set them manually on each text block. Here are two ways to speed this up.

Method 1: Create a text block with one blank space in it and maybe of couple of text characters. Apply the desired text style and spacing you want. Then either

- save it as a Library Object (covered later) or
- put it on a sample page at the end of the course where you either copy the text block or the entire page when needed.

Method 2. When you have some paragraphs that need the same spacing as others on the page, just copy and paste the hidden paragraph spacing. First click after the punctuation in a properly formatted paragraph. Drag right and you will get what looks like a blank space. Copy. Select the same on a paragraph where you want the same formatting. Paste. The target paragraph will now have the same spacing as the copy-from one.

Speed Tip 5: Get it right at the beginning.

As with anything, are many options on how things should look. Here is a Best Practice and a big time saver. Before you go too far, create several pages with different combinations, all with the same content. Then have several people review them including your boss, your course sponsor, and especially several potential learners. Get their input early rather than have to go back later and change 50-100 pages!

Using Text Styles

You can also set up text styles for certain types of text. Styles allow you to apply a set of font characteristics to text. If later you decide to change one of them, then you can change the style and that will in turn change all text where it is applied.

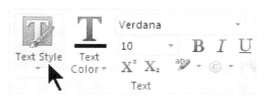

To create a style:

1. Click the Text Style icon and then click Manage Styles.

2. In the dialog box that appears, click New.

3. Specify the desired characteristics of the style and click OK.

4 To change a style, just click on it in the Manage Text Styles dialog box, click on the style you want to change, and then click Edit.

5. To apply a style to text, select the text and then click the Text Style icon and then click the desired style.

Warning 4: Styles in Lectora do *not* retain *paragraph* formatting (line spacing, between paragraph spacing, bullets) like styles do in MS Word®. Paragraph formatting must be changed in each paragraph manually so get it right early on.

Warning 5: Styles are global and apply to all titles you use. However, if you change a style, unlike MS Word®, it does *not* automatically change all the styles. Lectora will ask you if you want to change all the text. If you reply "Yes" it will change only the text in the current Title. It will not change:

- The text in other Titles

- Any text where the style has been applied *and* formatting has been changed. For example, if your Body style was 12 point Verdana and you bolded a word in a text block and then changed the style to 11 point, it would change all the text *except* the bolded word. That would still be 12 point bold.

If you do use styles, be sure to back them up from time to time by selecting them all in the Manage Text Styles window and clicking Export Styles.

Using Tables

Tables are an excellent way to present information in e-learning. Finding how to do this in Lectora can be a challenge.

1. Create a new text block. Make it a little bigger than the table you want.

2. Double click in text block where you want the table.

3. Click on the Table icon in either

   - the Add group on the Text Properties ribbon

   - or the Add Text group on the Insert ribbon and select the size table you want.

You will get a blank table with dotted lines around the cells to show you where the cells are. These dotted lines do *not* show when you publish your course.

4   To resize the table:
- first expand the text block;
- then double click inside the table;
- then, as you move your mouse-over the table edges, you will see the cursor change from an eyebeam to this: ⫟. That is when you can click and drag an edge.

5.   To add text to the table, all you have to do is double click in one of the cells.

Once you click inside the table, a new tab for the Table ribbon will appear.

Here you can format the table. The Include Header property is for web-based 508 compliance. See Lectora Help for more details.

On this ribbon, you can set a fixed row height, column width, border size, color, cell fill color, and objects are aligned in the cell. You can select more than one cell at a time and apply these properties. You select one of the preformatted table styles – a nice addition to Lectora 11.

 Warning 6: You can also set a cell margin however, unlike MS Word®, the margin applies *only* to the *left* and the *right*, *not* to the top and bottom of the cell. If you want more space above or below, you have to use Paragraph Spacing. (Yes, I know that is a little odd. Also, whatever space you set applies to both the left *and* the right margins. You cannot make them different from each other.

Finally, you can insert rows, columns, merge cells, split cells, and delete cells from the Edit Table dropdown list. They are only available when your cursor is in a table ready to enter text.

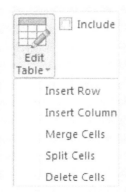

These functions are also available by right clicking when in a table and selecting Table.

The easiest way to add a row below the last row in a table is to click in the last row and press the Tab key until you are in the next row.

Design Guidelines for Tables

Here are some tips on creating professional looking tables.

Design Guideline 1: Black is the default color for table borders but *not* the best one to use. A better color is a medium or light shade of gray. It is less harsh and gives emphasis to the text rather than the table borders.

Here is a standard vanilla table with black lines and no shading. Looks fine but it can be better.

No.	Element	Symbol
1	Hydrogen	H
2	Helium	He

The next version has gray borders instead of black. Notice how it is a little easier on the eyes and places more emphasis on the content of the table.

No.	Element	Symbol
1	Hydrogen	H
2	Helium	He

The next two remove the vertical lines. It is now a bit more elegant and puts more emphasis on the rows.

No.	Element	Symbol
1	Hydrogen	H
2	Helium	He

Design Guideline 2: This table uses shaded rows for an even better effect.

This table has shaded rows and only a border around the outside giving more emphasis to the content. It also stands out more on the page. Shaded rows work especially well on wide tables.

No.	Element	Symbol
1	Hydrogen	H
2	Helium	He
3	Lithium	Li

Design Guideline 3: Keep columns a reasonable distance apart but not too much. About ¼ to ½ of an inch (25-50px) is a good start

Design Guideline 4: Use rounded numbers when detail is *not* needed.

Design Guideline 5: Put words before numbers except when numbering a list.

Using Tables for Special Bullets

Lectora can only create round bullets. You can use tables to create bulleted text. Here are two different uses of a table. The first uses something other than simple round bullets.

Here are some key points to remember:
- ✔ Checkmark bullet
- ✔ Next checkmark bullet

The second shows second level bullets. The dotted lines do not appear when seen by the learner.

- Here is the first bulletv.
- Next bullet goes here.
  - This is a second level bullet
  - Another second level bullet
- Back to another first level bullet.

Using Symbols

You can insert some of the more common symbols by clicking on the copyright icon on the home ribbon.

The More Symbols option at the bottom gives you a couple of more fonts to choose from.

If you want to use symbols from other fonts like Webdings or Wingdings, use the Windows® Character Map found somewhere under Programs > Accessories for Windows®.

 Best Practice 9: Be aware that not all computers will have these fonts so good practice is to check the Convert To Image property on the Text Properties ribbon.

☐ Wrap Text
☐ Vertical Scroll
☑ Convert To Image

Entering Math Equations

You can enter complex mathematical equations using the Equation Editor on the Insert Ribbon. This opens an Equation Editor and after that you are on your own.

Set the Text Block Properties

In addition to the how the text and paragraphs look, you can also do a lot with the entire block itself the same way you can color and put borders on text blocks in PowerPoint®.

Let's look at the most commonly used properties of a text block. Consult Lectora help to learn more about the other properties.

Help

First click on a text block to get to the Properties tab. Then click on the Properties tab.

The Wrap Text property enables text in a text block to flow around an overlapping object.

Lorem ipsum dolor sit amet, consect adipiscing elit, sed diem nonummy nibh euismod tincidunt ut lacreet dolore magna aliguam erat volutpat. Ut wisis

The Vertical Scroll property enables you to have more text that will show immediately. This sounds nice and is particularly useful when you need a text block that will contain the audio transcript. *However*, be aware that many people will not scroll down so if it is important, make it show when the page appears.

Lorem ipsum dolor sit amet, consect adipiscing elit, sed diem nonummy nibh euismod tinc dunt ut lacreet dolore magna aliguam erat volutpat. Ut wisis enim adminim

The Convert To Image property is useful when you are not sure that your viewing learners will have the fonts you used. However, be aware that text blocks with this property turned on are *not* 508 compliant.

The Background, Outline, Margin Size, Border Weight, and Border Style apply to the *entire* text block. With these, you can create a wide variety of effects for your text blocks. Currently there is no way to make one edge different from any of the others. Below are a few examples of the different border treatments.

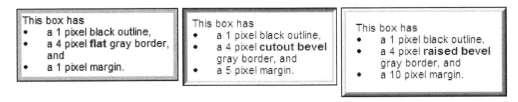

We will cover some of the other properties when we cover Transitions in Step 5: Make Things Happen.

Get the Spelling and Grammar Right

These are both important aspects of writing good e-learning courses. While Lectora does *not* have a grammar checker, there is sort of a workaround.

Check Your Spelling

Spell check is turned on by default on File menu > Preferences.

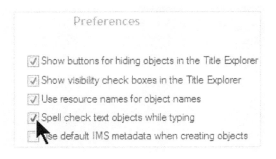

When this is turned on, spelling errors appear with a red wavy line under them when your cursor is in the text block.

Warning 7: Note that this only checks text while your cursor is an I-beam *inside* the text block. When your cursor is outside the text block, the red wavy lines do not appear.

bulletv.

You can also run spell check from the Tools ribbon. This will check all the text blocks, Display Message actions (discussed later), and question feedback.

Selecting Options from the dropdown list gives you a wide range of options for customizing the spell checker.

 Warning 8: Note that Spell Check does *not* check text in object names including Page names. If you use a template or an action (discussed later) that takes the Page name from the Title Explorer and puts it into a text block, you could have misspelled words that would *not* be caught.

Check Your Grammar

Okay, this is really not part of Lectora but Lectora does give you a way to catch really bad grammar errors.

1. Click on Export on the File ribbon. You will see you can export to MS Word®.

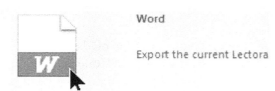

It only exports text, not graphics or anything else. It exports text blocks in the order they appear in the Title Explorer. Here the page title comes *after* the body text block.

When exported, they look like this →
with the title appearing *after* the body.

So, you might go to a bit of trouble to make sure the text blocks appear in the same sequence in the Title Explorer as they do in the layout pane – page title first and then the body text blocks in order.

Sample page body text. Lorem dolor sit amet, consect adipisc

Sample Page Title

2. Open this document with MS Word® and turn on your grammar checker. Then you can go through it and find any glaring grammar errors. Unfortunately, there is no good way to import them back into Lectora but at least you can make important changes manually. This is better than nothing.

Apply Design Guidelines for Easy-to-Read Pages

Design Guideline 1: Be consistent.

- The page number and navigation buttons should be in the same place and look the same throughout the course.

- The page title should be located at the same x,y coordinates on each page.

- I have found no evidence about whether the title should be centered or left justified. Pick one and stick with it. The body text blocks should be in the same location from page to page.

- The page title and body should use the same font face, color, etc.

Design Guideline 2: If you have instructions to learners, put instructions in bold or italics.

Examples:

Move your mouse over each block on the diagram for more information.

Move your mouse over each block on the diagram for more information.

Design Guideline 3: A good rule of thumb is to allow space for 100-150 words on a page not including the page title. The Gettysburg address contained 272 words; the FDA rules on cabbage are over 26,000. Need I say more?

Design Guideline 4: Limit the number of fonts used in a course to two, maybe three for special circumstances, unless you are explaining font usage.

Design Guideline 5: For narrow text blocks and very short wide text blocks of 3-4 lines, use the single line spacing. For long wide text blocks, increase the line spacing by one or two points as well as the paragraph spacing.

Design Guideline 6: Left justify text blocks leaving the right edge ragged. It is easier to read because computer fully justified text sometimes looks odd with unusual amounts of spacing. Fully justified text introduces excessive gaps between words, which sometimes make it difficult to read.

Design Guideline 7: The last line of each paragraph should have more than one word. While this is not always possible, give it your best shot.

Design Guideline 8: Try to avoid splitting paragraphs between columns or especially pages. When you must, avoid having just one line of the paragraph in a column or on a page by itself.

Design Guideline 9: Divide the body area into two vertical columns with about ¼ inch (25-35px) or more between them and the same amount of white space on each side. Look at newspapers, magazines, and other common media and you will see that the typical column width is usually between two and three inches. This makes it easy on the eyes to read. See the example on the following page.

Compare this version of a page with the text running all the way across the page

> ## Motivation vs. Attitude
>
> When supervising, it is important to separate motivation from attitude. Motivation is your drive to get the job done. Attitude is your feeling about something.
> An employee can have a good attitude (friendly to everyone and in a good mood) but not be motivated. An example is a very social employee who talks a lot more than working.
>
> An employee can display a poor attitude, but still be motivated to get the job done. An example of this is an employee who does not like the work, or who does not enjoy the people, but who enjoys the money or recognition that comes from the job.
>
> Before you begin to consider an employee's level of motivation, make sure you are not confusing it with his or her attitude. Ask questions to differentiate between the two:
>
> - What do you enjoy most about your job here?
> - What do you enjoy least about your job here? How does it make you feel?
> - If you could change two things about your job, what would you change and why?
> - What do you wish to be doing differently, if anything, in the next twelve months? Why?
> - Always focus on motivation, not attitude. Are your employees motivated to improve their performance?

to the one below using two columns shown next. The two-column version is generally considered *easier to read* because it is easier for the eyes to find the correct next line as they move down the page.

> ## Motivation vs. Attitude
>
> When supervising, it is important to separate motivation from attitude. Motivation is your drive to get the job done. Attitude is your feeling about something.
>
> An employee can have a good attitude (friendly to everyone and in a good mood) but not be motivated. An example is a very social employee who talks a lot more than working.
>
> An employee can display a poor attitude, but still be motivated to get the job done. An example of this is an employee who does not like the work, or who does not enjoy the people, but who enjoys the money or recognition that comes from the job.
>
> Before you begin to consider an employee's level of motivation, make sure you are not confusing it with his or her attitude. Ask questions to differentiate between the two:
>
> - What do you enjoy most about your job here?
> - What do you enjoy least about your job here? How does it make you feel?
> - If you could change two things about your job, what would you change and why?
> - What do you wish to be doing differently, if anything, in the next twelve months? Why?
> - Always focus on motivation, not attitude. Are your employees motivated to improve their performance?

Use Advanced Techniques

Even with all the above, you may still want to do more like use Cascading Style Sheets, translate your course or even have a way to easily change the text *after* publishing.

Do You Need Advanced Formatting?

Lectora allows you to insert HTML, Cascading Style Sheets (CSS), and JavaScript if you are publishing your course for viewing with a browser. These are advanced capabilities covered in *Lectora 301: Techniques for Professionals*. That book covers how to use them with Lectora but not the details of any of how to write HTML, CSS, or JavaScript. You can buy books on each of them and a good place to start for free online tutorials is:

www.w3schools.com

Click on the diagonal arrow in the Appearance group on the properties for any object to specify one or more a CSS Classes to apply to this object.

Do You Need to Translate Your Course?

Will your course be translated into other languages? If so, you can use the Translations tool in the Manage group of the Tools ribbon. This will export the text from your course to a Rich Text File (RTF).

You can then have translators translate the text using a MS WordPad. For more on translation, see Appendix 2: Translation Tips.

Do You Need Text Changes *After* Publishing?

Sometimes you will know when you are creating your course that some text in the course is subject to frequent change. Things like who to contact and contact information are examples. Depending on your needs, there are two ways to do this. You can use the Dynamic Text capability or you can use inserted RTF or TXT documents.

Using Dynamic Text

Dynamic Text allows you to update specific text in a Title published for viewing in a browser without republishing the Title. Lectora Help says,

This means that you can then change the text in dyntytle.xml and when the course is opened the new text will be displayed. Of course, you have to be sure the text will fit in the space allowed in the course.

1. First, check the Enable Dynamic Text Option on the Title options of the Design ribbon.

2. On each of the text blocks you want to be able to change, check Dynamic Text in the Web Options group of the Properties ribbon.

3. After the course is published, you can go to the dyntitle.xml file and change the text. Your changes will appear in the text blocks when the course is launched.

   This enables you to either change the text for a given course or easily have multiple versions of the same course launched from different folders.

The XML file is named *dyntitle.xml*. When the published title is displayed in a browser, text within the title is substituted with text found within *dyntitle.xml*.

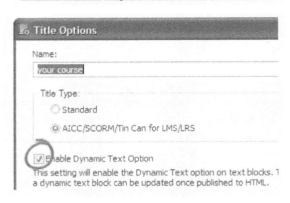

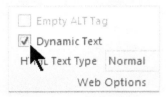

Using RTF or TXT Documents

You can create either Rich Text File (RTF) documents or just plain text documents and view them from a course page.

Lorem ipsum dolor sit amet, consect adipiscing elit, sed diem nonummy nibh euismod tincidunt ut lacreet dolore magna aliguam erat volutpat. Ut wisis enim adm nim veniam, quis nostrud exerci tution ullam corper suscipit

- You can change the content after the course is published.

- You can use the same document in multiple places in the course. For example: a case study that is revisited several times.

They work when published as a single file executable and HTML. Here is all you do.

1. Create your document using NotePad, MS WordPad, or even MS Word®. The file type must be TXT or RTF, not DOCX.

2. Drag and drop it onto the page where you want it.

3. Resize and position the window as needed.

Now, any time you change the document, the changes appear when the course is viewed.

4. If you set MS WordPad as the Documents editor in on the File menu,

Preferences

The following editors will be launched when the Edit button object's Property window.

Images:	
Audio:	C:\Program Files\Trivantis\Lectora Publish
Video:	C:\Program Files\Trivantis\Lectora Publish
Animations:	
Documents:	C:\Program Files\Windows NT\Accessori
Text Files:	C:\WINDOWS\Notepad.exe

then you can edit the document by simply right-clicking on it and selecting Edit or clicking on the Edit icon on the Properties ribbon.

The biggest downside to the documents is that there is no way to control the border that surrounds the text on the page unless you use CSS.

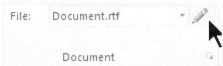

File: Document.rtf

Document

Practice What You Learned

You learned a lot about adding text to your course. Before going on, take some time to create a few more pages and apply these techniques. Experiment with different options. This way what you have learned will stay with you.

Then be sure you show some of the sample pages to your stakeholders and get their ideas. This way you don't develop the whole course and find that someone wants to change something that would have been easy if they had suggested it early on.

Remember These Key Points

- Clean out the unnecessary objects if you use templates or themes.

- Paste text from other sources using Paste Unformatted to avoid embedding hidden characters that will bite you later.

- Use Styles whenever possible to format text. Then when you need to change all the text with that style, it is easy.

- Use tables if you need specialized bullets.

- Text blocks can have their own background color and borders as needed.

- Spell check using Lectora. Export to MS Word® to grammar check.

- Review the Design Guidelines in this step after you have created several pages and make the necessary adjustments.

- Dynamic text is helpful if you have text that is likely to change.

Remember, if you want the Lectora Title that I used to create this book with **working examples**, go to www.eProficiency.com/101.html.

Step 4: Increase Interest and Retention

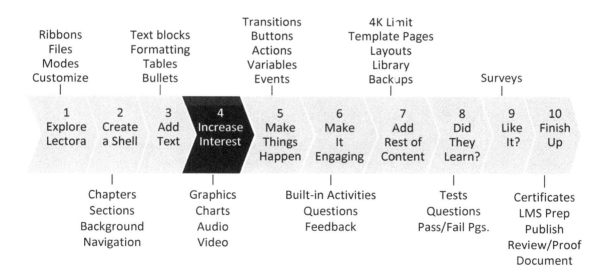

Text can get boring after a while. In this step and the next, you will learn ways to make your course more interesting.

Here are some things you can do to liven up your course.

Use Graphics	Paste in *relevant* pictures and graphics. Add some color.
Use Tables and Charts	If you have data that fits either tables or charts, these are great ways to make your information easier to understand and remember.
Add Audio	Audio is *not* good for *everything* and some people seriously overuse it, but it can add depth, interest, and really increase learning and retention when used correctly.
Add Animations	Flash and the like can be very helpful when it comes to explaining how thing work. The downside is it usually takes a large amount of effort to develop them in Flash or similar tools.
Add Video	If you want to make an important point, use video. If you over use it, learners will get bored in a hurry.
Make It Eye-appealing	Just throwing things on a page can give the wrong impression and take away from learning. Learn and use these guidelines and tools for a professional look.
Find things	Once you get rolling, it helps if you can find where you used things. That is what you learn how to do here.

Use Graphics to Aid Learning

An excellent source of how to use graphics to enhance learning is *Graphics for Learning* by Clark & Lyons (2004). If you are not already familiar with the material in this book, I highly recommend it for the best use of graphics. It is not just someone's opinion; it is based on solid research.

You can add two basic types of static graphics to your course – Lectora shapes and external images.

Inserting Lectora Shapes

You can insert a variety of basic shapes with Lectora's drawing tool. Just click on the Shape/Line icon on the Insert ribbon and select the shape you want.

Then click on your page and draw your shape.

(Note that shapes in Lectora cannot contain text. If you want text on your shape, create a text block and place it in front of the shape.)

To change the color, or outline properties, click on the shape and then on the Properties ribbon. Change the shape's color and size in the Style group.

When you change a color anywhere in Lectora, after clicking on the color icon, you get dropdown selection window.

- You can select any one of the standard colors. These are not changeable like they are in PowerPoint®.

- You can click on one of the Recent colors.

- You can click on Custom which brings up a dialog window where you can specify the exact RBG color.

- You can click on Select and use the eyedropper to match any color currently on your screen simply by clicking on it.

Best Practice 10: Limit your colors for basic shapes on a given page to 3-4 not counting your logo.

Best Practice 11: Use a consistent color scheme throughout your course. Pick a set of colors 3-4 and use them for borders, shading, etc. You can use shades of those colors but even so, limit the number of variations.

Time *is* Money

Speed Tip 6: To easily implement your color scheme, create one small rectangle for each color you plan to use. Put these together at the top of your course. Set the Always on Top and Hidden properties so you can always get to them while editing but they will not show when you run the course. Then when you need one of the colors, you just select the eyedropper and click on the color you need.

These colors will soon appear in the Recent colors area so you may not need them as long as you stick with a limited set of colors.

One big reason for using this technique is that the Recent colors change when you work on another course with a different set of colors. If you rely on the Recent color list, the ones for the current course will be gone when you come back to it.

You can search the internet for color scheme generators. I like www.colorschemedesigner.com.

Time *is* Money

Speed Tip 7: Use the Shift key to speed up drawing.

- Hold the Shift key down when you draw a shape to get it to have the same height and width (square, circle).

Shift

- Do the same when resizing to maintain the current size ratio of width to height.

- Hold the Shift key down when drawing a line to get either a horizontal, vertical, or 45° diagonal line.

Using External Images – Pictures and Drawings from Other Applications

You can use all sorts of pictures and graphics created with other software. There are four types that are used frequently with Lectora. We cover those first and then show you how to insert graphics (or images as Lectora calls them). Then we cover some ideas on where you can get ready-made graphics (some for free), and some guidelines about using graphics.

About Image File Types

Here are the four most popular file types (or formats). For more information on these and other graphic types, see http://en.wikipedia.org/wiki/Image_file_formats.

GIF	Graphics Interchange Format
	– The original file format for the Internet
	– Limited colors (256 colors)
	– Low quality transparency
	– Works reliably on all browsers
	– Can be animated
JPG or JPEG	Joint Photographic Experts Group
	– Uses 24 bit color (16+ million colors)
	– Usually a good choice for pictures
	– No transparency
PNG	Portable Network Graphics
	– Png24 uses 24 bit color (16+ million colors)
	– Usually a good choice for pictures
	– Png32 upports high-quality transparency for most browsers except IE6.
BMP	Windows® bitmap
	– Uses 24 bit color (16+ million)
	– No transparency
	– Usually is the largest file size

On the next page is a comparison of the different formats. The columns are shaded to emphasize transparency which is not obvious when the objects are placed on a white background. Notice that the GIF versions are generally lower quality.

Regardless of the file type, you only need a resolution of 96DPI or PPI (dots per inch or pixels per inch) for computer screens because that is all they currently display. Windows systems use 96PPI while Macs use 72PPI.

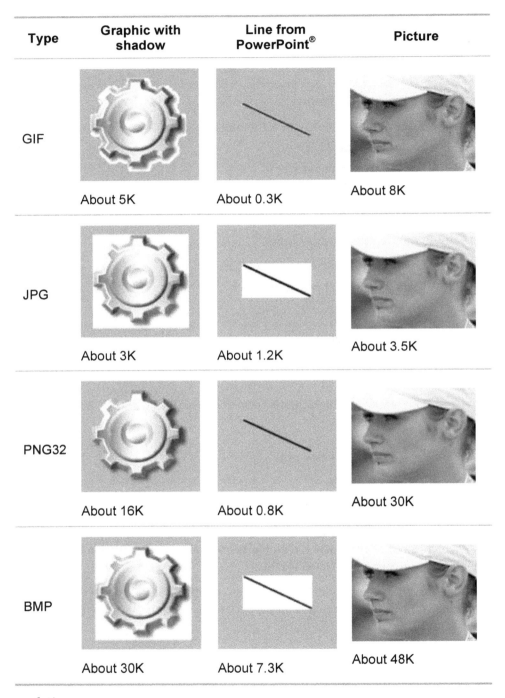

Type	Graphic with shadow	Line from PowerPoint®	Picture
GIF	About 5K	About 0.3K	About 8K
JPG	About 3K	About 1.2K	About 3.5K
PNG32	About 16K	About 0.8K	About 30K
BMP	About 30K	About 7.3K	About 48K

Recommendations:

- Use JPG for most pictures and graphics when transparency is not needed.
- Use PNG32 when transparency is needed.
- Avoid PNG8 because it is much like a GIF.

Inserting Graphics

There are several ways you can add graphics to your course.

Copy and Paste	You can copy the graphic from a drawing tool and paste it into Lectora. Usually it will go in as a BMP file which is the largest. When your course is published, Lectora will convert it to a JPG or PNG to reduce the file size. You can also right click on the Lectora page and select **Paste As** and the most appropriate format. If you are coming from PowerPoint®, your JPGs and PNGs will become bigger in width and height. You may have to reduce them in PowerPoint® before copying. Another alternative is to use SnagIt.
Drag and Drop	You can open a folder in Windows® Explorer that contains your graphics and just drag and drop them on to the page. Then move them to where you want them. Remember, if you need to resize them, do that *before* you put them in Lectora for best results.
Use the Insert ribbon	You can click on the Image icon in the **Add Image** group on the **Insert** ribbon and select one of the choices.

Graphics Sources

While Lectora does have some drawing capability, most developers use some sort of drawing tool like Photoshop® or PowerPoint®. If you need some pictures or other graphics, search these sites for graphics. The first two seem to be free. In all cases, read the usage agreements posted on the website. There are probably many other sources out there.

office.Microsoft.com/en-us/clipart/	www.fotalia.co.uk
www.morguefile.com	www.istockphoto.com
www.sxc.hu	www.photosights.net
www.photos.com	www.fotosearch.com
www.alamy.com	www.copyrightfreephotos.com
www.clipart.com	www.photolibrary.com
www.everystockphoto.com	www.flickr.com
www.shutterstock.com	www.jupiterimages.com
www.elearningart.com	www.narratorfiles.com

Here is how I go looking for ready-made graphics.

1. Open office.Microsoft.com/en-us/clipart/ and www.morguefile.com and enter the word.

2. Open www.google.com > images and enter the word or phrase. These are not free but you can get some very good ideas.

3. If I don't find what I want, I go to www.thesaurus.com and enter a word for the kind of graphic I am looking for. Then use the synonyms to search in the other three browser windows.

Graphics Design Guidelines

Design Guideline 1: Make sure that you highlight important information (arrows, circles, etc.).

Design Guideline 2: Keep your graphics as simple as possible. The more that you show, the more effort it takes to understand. Sometimes simple line drawings are better than actual photographs because the photographs show too much detail.

Design Guideline 3: Make sure they are large enough to see any pertinent information.

Design Guideline 4: Place your graphics near the text they apply to. For example, instead of numbering parts of a diagram and having numbered text explanations above or below the diagram as in A below, put the explanations right next to the respective parts of the diagram as in B or C.

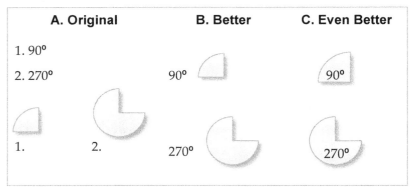

Design Guideline 5: When feasible, use audio to explain graphic models, animations, and diagrams. It results in better learning than using text because it uses a different channel into the brain (auditory vs. visual).

Design Guideline 6: Show flows and time from left to right or top to bottom for western cultures (Americas and Europe).

Design Guideline 7: If your graphic does not add to the instruction, *then it* *detracts* because learners have to spend time figuring out how it relates to the text. Look for graphics that:

Represent the topic such as the picture of a tool in a lesson on engine maintenance

Organize the topic such as an organization diagram or a process flowchart

Show changes over time or space including time-line diagrams, before and after pictures, and time-lapse videos

Make invisible concepts visible such as drawings of atoms, molecules, pressure, heat, wind currents

In other words, avoid the regular use of decorative graphics that may make the page look nice or add humor but do not help explain anything. Research has shown that these actually *take away from the effectiveness of the course. Test your graphics. If you can delete the graphic and the only impact is that the page is a little bare, then delete the graphic.* Ruth Clark in many of her books has research that proves this. "Not only did the interesting (but irrelevant) visuals not improve learning—they actually disrupted the formation of the desired mental models and consequently depressed learning!" (2008a, p. 39).

Design Guideline 8: Give pictures a border of some kind or a shadow to make them look more professional. Notice in the examples below how the right two treated pictures look a little more professional. These treatments were done using PowerPoint®® 2007 so you do not need to know some special drawing tool like PhotoShop® to do this. And, using PowerPoint®'s Format Painter found on the left of the Home ribbon, you can easily apply the same affect to multiple pictures.

No border   Soft/faded edge   Border & shadow

> **Design Guideline 9:** Give the *same* kind of treatment to all pictures unless there is a good reason not to.

Getting Objects Layered Right

Now that you have some graphics text blocks on pages, you may find that they overlap from time to time. Sometimes you will have several objects in the same place on the screen and only show one of them at a time such as different feedback text blocks depending on how the learner answers a question. When objects on a page overlap, they form layers – some are in front of others. This is called "layering."

How Lectora Decides Which Objects Are in Front

When a page is constructed by a browser (or rendering program) it puts items on the page *in the order that they appear in the* Title Explorer. As it starts to create the page from the information sent to it, it starts at the top of the Title Explorer and puts the objects on the page as it encounters them. This way the first items down end up behind the ones that come later.

Example: It's like cards off the top of a deck and dealing them out. The cards on the top of the deck go on the table first. They are covered up by the cards farther down the deck.

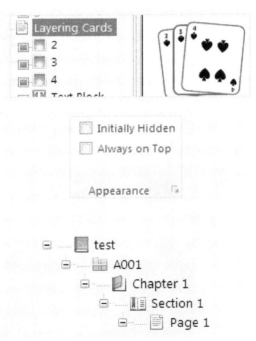

When a page is presented to the learner, two rendering passes over the Lectora content take place.

The **first** pass selects objects that do *not* have the Always on Top property checked.

- Title level objects are placed on the screen beginning with the *top* in the Title Explorer.

- Assignable Unit objects go on top of them in the same sequence.

- Chapter level objects are next followed by Section and Page level objects.

In the example shown here, the blue header appears behind both the Breadcrumb and the Course Title. If the Breadcrumb and the Course Title text blocks overlapped, the Course Title would be in front of the Breadcrumb. This way, if you have background objects for the Title or Chapter, any overlapping ones on the Page will appear in front of them.

Now, suppose you have some objects like navigation buttons at the Title level that you want to be sure are on top of things on the Page.

That is when you use the Always on Top property.

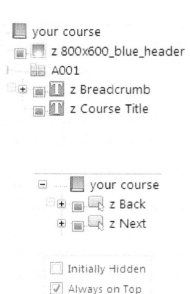

In the **second** pass the rendering application selects objects that *do have* the Always on Top property checked. These objects are placed in front of any first pass objects in the same way as first pass objects were layered.

- Title level objects go on first from the top in the Title Explorer down to the first AU/Chapter/ Section or Page.

- Assignable Unit objects go on top of them in the same sequence.

- Then Chapter level objects are next followed by Section level objects and then the objects on the page.

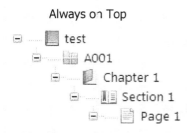

How You Can Control Which Objects Are in Front

To move object to the front or to the back within a given level (Title, AU, Chapter, Section, Page) you can do one of the following:

- Right click on the object and select the desired movement.

- In the Title Explorer, drag the object
  - up to move it behind other objects or
  - down to move it forward.

How to Work with Objects That Are Behind Other Objects

When you are working with the object on the front layer, it is easily visible. You can just click on it and do what needs to be done. But when you want to work with an object that is *behind* another one, you have to do something to bring it to the top to work on.

1. On the File ribbon > Preferences, check the Show visibility check box.

2. Clear the box to the left of the object in the Title Explorer. This will hide the object from view in the layout area so you can see the object behind it.

   This hides the object for editing purposes only. It will still appear on the screen when your course is run.

Best Practice 12: Use the Always on top property as a *last resort* because if you have it on all your objects there will come a day when you need it and you have already used it. Try your best to control laying by bringing objects to the front or sending them to the back before you resort to Always on top.

Creating a Custom Background

You have several ways you can create a background for your course pages. You can:

- Create a single image the exact size of a typical course page and tell Lectora to use it by clicking on the Image icon and navigating to it. If you background covers the entire page, this is better than just having it at the Title level because it will not be selected when you click on a blank page.

- Place your graphics like the Themes do in a group at the top level of your course. This way the graphics are easily changeable but you can accidently select them when selecting things on the page. If they are locked, they will not move but it is still a pain because you have re-do your selection.

- If you have slightly different backgrounds in different parts of your courses, you can combine the two methods. You can have a background image that has the common elements and then place the unique ones at the Chapter or Section level for each unique area.

Make Things Clear with Tables and Charts

Simply presenting paragraph after paragraph or bullet after bullet of text does not always do a good job of helping the learner understand what you are trying to communicate. Tables and charts present information in a way that may be easier to understand and remember.

Using Tables

Tables are an excellent way to present information, especially if you want to compare items. Details on tables are covered in the step on Text in Using Tables on page 57.

Using Charts

Charts are another good way to present information. To add a chart in Lectora, click the Chart
icon in the Add Image group of the Insert ribbon.
This opens up a dialog window where you can
select the chart type and enter the data.

On the Title & Legend tab you can change the font
characteristics of the title and legend.

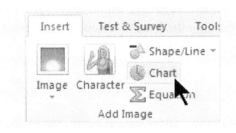

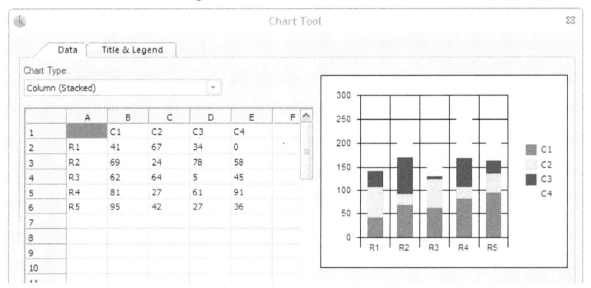

Unfortunately, at the current time (April 2013) there does not appear to be a way to change the
colors in the chart. It may make more sense to create the chart in PowerPoint®, Excel, or MS
Word® where you have much more control over the format of the chart and then copy and paste
it here.

> **Design Guideline 1:** Make sure both the vertical and horizontal axes are la-
> beled.
>
> **Design Guideline 2:** Three-dimensional charts may look cool but are harder to
> interpret than flat ones (Lohr, 2008, p. 141). Compare these two charts. It is
> harder in the 3D one to tell exactly how high the bars are. Some of the granulari-
> ty of the vertical axis was lost when it was converted to 3D. The value for the
> year 2000 is 4 in both but note that the 3D one appears to be slightly less.

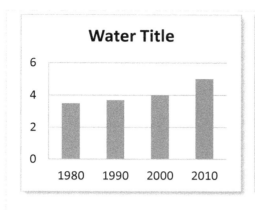 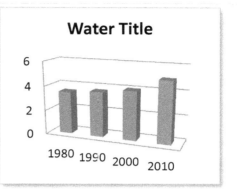

(Note that both have poorly labeled vertical axes.)

Use Audio for the Right Stuff

Be judicious about using audio in your course.
Use audio:

- for learners who have difficulty reading text or

- to describe complex graphics

- to provide emotional impact when teaching interpersonal/emotional topics.

Do not put audio on every page. Seems strange but I feel obligated to start off with a story and a warning about using audio because I see it so often abused.

> **Experience may be the best teacher, but it is expensive!**
>
> I once was asked to develop a course with audio on *every* page. The audio tracks averaged around 2 minutes with some up to 3.5 minutes. The pages contained text only, no diagrams relating to the audio. Learners ended up being bored to death. Some usability tests found the learner zoning out after 5-10 pages of this and retaining very little. A few pages with audio would have been fine to emphasize a point and add variety. But too much of a good thing …

Warning 9: Research by Ruth Clark (2003, p. 93) has shown that "presenting words in **both text and audio narration can hurt learning.**" That's right, *hurt* learning. The only time you should have the same words as you have in the audio is when you must accommodate hearing impaired learners. If you need to do this, make the text optional—available by clicking a button.

Guidelines for Using Audio

Use these guidelines when you are considering using audio in your course.

Design Guideline 1: Provide a way for visual learners to turn the audio off and read the script if you are not describing a graphic. This will help motivate your visual learners.

Design Guideline 2: Be aware that proofing your course will take longer. Someone will have to listen to the audio and compare it to the script. There is no way to hurry that along.

Design Guideline 3: Do *not* use audio when learners will have to refer to the content as in an exercise. Use text instead.

Design Guideline 4: Be sure that all learners will have the ability to listen to the audio and that it will not interfere with others in the workplace.

Design Guideline 5: Provide learner controls to pause and replay the audio.

Design Guideline 6: Keep it short. Two minutes is a good maximum length. As the audio gets longer, learners' attention tends to wander and the impact of the audio diminishes.

Design Guideline 7: Use a human voice, not one that sounds computer-generated.

Recording Audio

Lectora provides a couple of ways you can record audio as long as you have a microphone on your computer.

- You can select New Audio Recording from the Audio dropdown list on the Insert ribbon.

- From the Tools ribbon, you can click on Audio Recording.

- You can open the Audio Editor by right clicking on any existing audio file and selecting Edit. There you can click on the record button next to the controller. It will open a dialog window where you can record your audio. You must have a microphone on your computer for this to work.

Design Guideline 8: If things change, you may have to rerecord the audio. Make sure you will have the time and budget to do that and that the voice talent will be available.

Design Guideline 9: Make the volume consistent. Be sure to hold the microphone at the same distance from your mouth and talk using the same volume. A headset helps with this.

Design Guideline 10: Make sure all background sounds have been eliminated.

> **Experience may be the best teacher, but it is expensive!**
>
> I once listened to a course and you could hear a train going through in the background now and then. Turned out that the recorder lived near a train track and had gotten so used to the sound he did not even notice it any more.

Inserting Audio

You can insert audio by simply dragging and dropping audio files onto your Lectora page or you can click the audio button on the Insert ribbon and navigate to the folder where you have your audio files.

Lectora adds the audio to the media folder for your course.

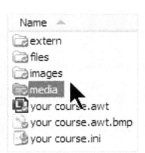

Once you have the audio file inserted and selected, you have access to the audio Properties.

If you want to change the audio file used, you can select a different audio file using the Audio dropdown box in the Audio group.

Now, make your selections in the Playback Options group.

1. If you want the audio to start playing as soon as the page shows up, click Auto Start.

2. If you want it to repeat, click Loop.

3. Specify how you want the audio file to look on the screen. You can:
   - hide it completely by selecting None,
   - use an icon, which allows the learner to play/pause the audio, or
   - select an audio controller.

   If your audio is over 5-10 seconds, then a controller is probably your best choice.

4. If you select Controller, the Controller icon be-
    comes available and you can select from a long
    list of audio controllers. These allow the learn-
    er to play, pause, and replay the audio as well
    as see how much more there is to go.

Closed Captioning

You can add closed captioning to your audio. This topic is advanced and is covered in *Lectora 301: Techniques for Professionals.*

Converting Audio

1. Note that some file types like WAV allow
    you to select a controller using the Display
    icon *but only one controller* is available.
    When you have clicked on these types of
    audio files, the Controller icon is grayed out
    but there is a new property, Convert to
    MP3. You can click it and Lectora will con-
    vert your file to MP3 file format. This will
    give you a wide range of controllers as
    well as the ability to control things hap-
    pening on the screen as the audio plays.

2. When the convert dialog window opens,
    select a low to medium level of compres-
    sion to start with. You can experiment
    with other levels of compression. Be sure
    to preview them in a browser before set-
    tling on a final level.

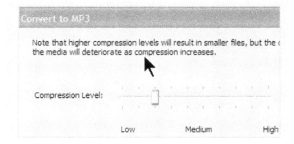

Editing Audio

When you click on the Edit button on its Properties ribbon or right click on the audio object
and select Edit, it brings up an audio file editor
where you can:

- cut and paste parts of the audio,

- fade parts in or out,

- adjust the volume,

- insert silence, or

- add events.

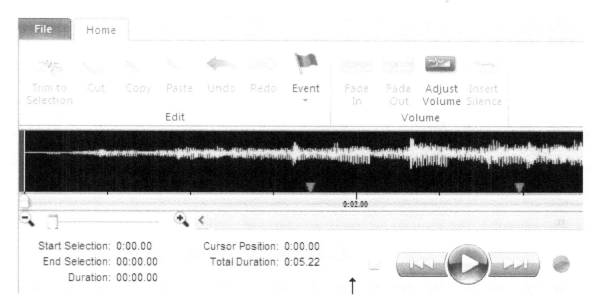

To select a portion of the audio, simply click in the black area and drag your cursor. You can also
hold the Shift key down and click. The area selected will be from the current play position to
where you clicked.

Once you have a selected area, you can delete everything but the selection using Trim to Selection.
You can Cut, Copy, Fade, Adjust Volume, or silence the recording.

You can also make things appear or disappear as the audio is playing. We cover how to do this in
the next step.

Grab Their Attention with Animations

Animations are a great way to grab the learner's attention and make your point. Here are some of
the best times to use them:

- On the first page of the course sometimes called the "splash" page

- When you want to make a very important point

- When you are explaining how something works like a diagram that shows the flow of materials through a machine

Animations are essentially computer drawn objects moving around on the screen. They fall into two broad classes in Lectora.

Animating Static Objects	This class takes a static object such as a picture, graphic, or even a text block on the screen and makes it "move."
Self-contained Animations	Today the two main forms of self-contained animations are animated GIFs and Flash-based animations (SWFs) created in Flash, FlyPaper, Captivate, etc. You can also do things within Lectora

Animating Static Objects

There are three ways to make static objects "move" in Lectora.

1. Use one of the Transition properties associated with a graphic covered in Step 5: Make Things Happen.

2. Use "pose-able" characters covered in Step 5: Make Things Happen.

3. Use a MoveTo or SizeTo actions in Lectora covered in *Lectora 301: Techniques for Professionals*.

Inserting Animated GIFs

1. Insert animated GIFs by clicking on the Animation icon on the Insert ribbon.

2. Select one of the two choices.

   - If you select Animation File, you navigate to the folder where your animated GIF is and select it.

   - If you select My Animation, Lectora opens the Media Library and you can select a Library Object.

3. Then move it to the desired location on your page.

4. By default, animated GIFs have their **Auto Start** property set. If you want to start it when something else happens on the screen, uncheck this property and use a **Play** action. (See Creating Your Own Play and Pause Buttons on page 137.)

Inserting Flash Animations (SWFs)

Lectora provides you with some moderately animated Flash objects which include some that simply move and others that require the user to do something, usually answer questions and then things happen based on the answer. Some use a single audio file and others use multiple audio files where you can time text bullets to show fairly easily as the audio plays.

1. Insert Flash animations by clicking on the **Flash** icon on the **Insert** ribbon.

2. Select one of the three choices.
   – If you select **Flash File**, you navigate to the folder where your Flash file is and select it.
   – If you select **My Flash**, Lectora opens the Media Library and you can select a **Library Object**.
   – If you select **Flash Activity**, Lectora opens the Stock Library where you can select one of many built-in Flash animations. It then gives you a dialog window where you can set the parameters for that animation.

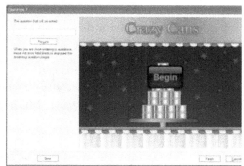

3. Check the **Transparent** property if you have anything you want to show through the Flash object like a start or stop button. Otherwise, it will be in front of objects that have the **Always on top** property checked.

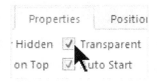

4. If you used one of the Lectora provided Flash animations and need to make changes, click on the **Flash Parameters** icon.

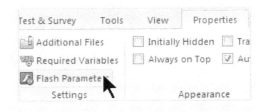

This opens a window where you can set the parameters.

5. As with other windows like this, you can delete rows by clicking on the ⊝.

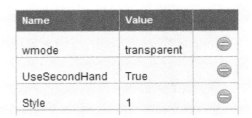

6. You may want to change other settings using the **Additional Files** or **Required Variables** properties if your custom Flash animation requires it.

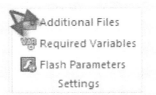

7. That will open a wizard window where you specify the many options for the activity. When you are done, you can see how it looks by clicking the **Run** mode button at the bottom of the screen.

In general, Flash animations can be resized, especially made smaller. Be sure to check how they look once published to HTML before you go too far.

 Warning 10: While easy to set up, these activities do have several limitations:

- There is no controller so the learner cannot easily backup or replay it.
- The Flash commands like **Play**, **Pause**, and **Stop** or the **Flash Commands** may or may not work depending on the animation. Some work in **Run** mode but not when published to Web (HTML) or SCORM.
- For some, an **On Done Playing** action fires immediately so you can't have things happen when the activity is finished.
- If the animation wizard has you input text, spellcheck does not check the text.

Drive Home Important Points with Video

Videos are another a great way to grab the learner's attention and make your point. Here are some of the best times to use them:

- On the first page of the course sometimes called the "splash" page. Have the president of the company or a subject matter expert welcome the person to the course

- When you want to make a very important point

- When you are explaining how something works like

  - a diagram that shows the flow of materials through a machine or

  - someone performing a task

- When you are trying to teach interpersonal skills like communication or supervision

- When your course is attempting to change attitudes

Using Video Effectively

Use these guidelines when you are considering using video in your course.

Design Guideline 1: Allow extra time to proof your course. Someone will have to watch the video and compare it to the script. There is no way to hurry that along.

Design Guideline 2: Be sure that all learners will have the ability to listen to the audio and that it will not interfere with others in the workplace.

Design Guideline 3: Provide learner controls to pause and replay the video.

Design Guideline 4: Use video for important information, *not* for unimportant information.

Design Guideline 5: Do *not* use video where audio or text alone would suffice. In other words, avoid talking heads or video for the sake of having something different. Learners will focus some part of their attention on the visual aspects of the video and that will detract from learning the content.

Design Guideline 6: Keep it short. Two minutes is a good maximum length—30 seconds is better. As they get longer, the learners' attention tends to wander and the impact of the video diminishes.

Recording Video

You can record your own video using Lectora but I don't recommend it. The qualities of most computer cameras (webcams) as well as the *recording environment* are *not* conducive to producing high quality video recordings.

Lectora provides a couple of ways you can record audio as long as you have a microphone and a webcam on your computer.

- You can select New Video Recording from the Video dropdown list on the Insert ribbon

- From the Tools ribbon, you can click on Audio Recording.

- You can open the Audio Editor by right clicking on any existing audio file and selecting Edit. There you can click on the record button next to the controller. It will open a dialog window where you can record your audio. You must have a microphone on your computer for this to work.

Inserting Video

1. Insert video by clicking on the Video icon in the Add Media group on the Insert ribbon.

2. Select one of the options from the dropdown list.

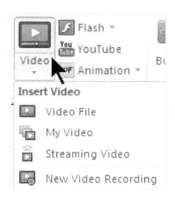

- If you select a video file, the file will be added to the media folder for your course.

- If you select Streaming Video, Lectora opens a dialog window where you can enter the URL of your streaming video.

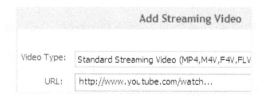

3. You can also insert a link to a YouTube video by clicking on the YouTube icon. This will open a dialog window where you can enter the desired URL.

Editing Video

Once a video file is inserted, you can edit it, change the controller, convert to MP4, or add captions (MP4 only) in much the same way you can audio by clicking on the Edit icon in the Properties ribbon or right-clicking on it and selecting Edit from the dropdown list.

Making Sure They Paid Attention

Okay, this is not a book on e-learning instructional design, but this is just a heads up. Have you ever watched videos in a training course? Some are pretty boring and yet contain some important information. Yet learners frequently start watching and then zone out. So what can you do? Here are a couple of techniques you can use to make your videos more effective.

- Ask questions before the video starts and tell them that there will be a pop quiz after the video is over.

- Stop the video in the middle and ask a question.

- After it is over, ask several questions on the content.

Guidelines and Tools for Professional Page Layout

By now you probably have several pages created with many different objects. Page layout is a very important aspect of developing your course. Think about a typical textbook. There are many cues and conventions used.

- The first Page in each Chapter usually has a special look to let you know you are starting a new Chapter.

- Where things are on each page is generally consistent from page to page so you know where to look for things.

- Headings at the very top of the page are always in the same place using the same font.

- Columns are usually the same width and in the same place.

- Topic headings are different sizes and styles to cue you to the level of the topic.

Let's look at a few design guidelines before we get into how to put them into effect.

Design Guideline 1: Keep objects (blocks to text, graphics, pictures, buttons) that belong together, close to each other.

Design Guideline 2: Use additional white space to separate groups of objects rather than lines or a grid like a table, which add clutter to your page.

Design Guideline 3: If you have text and a short graphic, try to balance the two so that they are roughly the same height. If the graphic is a lot shorter than the text column, try putting at least three lines of text under the graphic. You are not locked into this layout; it is just a good guideline for most pages.

- Align multiple objects (text blocks, graphics) using the alignment tools. If you have just a text block and a graphic, then it usually looks nice to have the tops or centers aligned. If you have multiple graphics, align them somehow – centers, left edges, top edges, etc. Try several to see which looks best.

Design Guideline 4: If the photo contains a face, have it face the text it relates to.

Design Guideline 5: If you have 2 or 3 pictures on a page, try to:

- Make them the same height if they are side by side or the same width if they are stacked.

- Give them the same treatment (shadow, border).

- Align them.

Design Guideline 6: Remember, "Less is more [effective]." Don't crowd your pages with lots of information or graphics. It confuses learners and takes away from their mastering the material. They spend time and energy trying to figure out what the page is all about or what is important rather than understanding and remembering what you are trying to get across.

Lectora provides you with several tools to lay out your pages easily and implement these design guidelines. Using them will give your pages a more professional look.

Using Grids and Guides

The Grids and the Guides are available on the View ribbon. They help you arrange things on the page and be consistent from page to page. They do not show once the course is published. Most people use one or the other, not both.

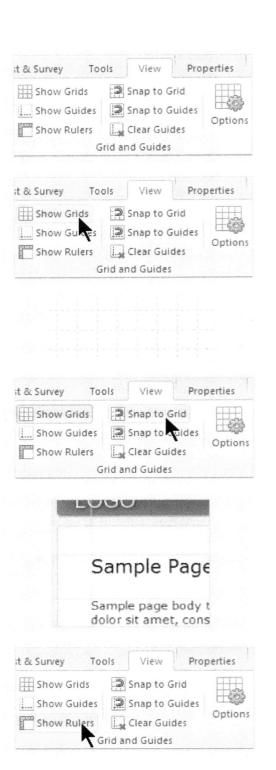

1   Click Show Grids to show the grid on the screen. You can change the color of the grids and how far they are apart by clicking on the Options icon.

Your screen will have a light grid which will help you align text blocks and graphics.

2.   At this point, they are just a visual aid. Objects will not "snap" to them. To get that to happen, you have to click Snap to Grid. Now when you drag an object close to a grid line, it will stick until you have gone well past the line.

Guides are similar to the guides in PowerPoint® – a few horizontal and vertical lines that you set where you want them. Then you use them to make sure things such as the title and the body text are in the same place on every page.

To set your Guides, you first have to show the rulers.

1.   Click on Show Rulers on the View ribbon.

2. Then click inside a ruler and drag onto the page. You should see something like this. Drop where you want the guide.

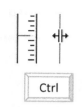

3. If you want to move the ruler, hold the Ctrl key down and move your mouse over it. When it changes to a double-sided arrow like the one you see here, click and drag the guide.

4. Once you have the guides where you want them, you can turn off the rulers by clicking Show Rulers again.

5. The default color for your guides is a bright blue. A better choice that interferes less when you are laying out the page is a medium gray. To change the guide color, click on the Options icon and change it to a gray.

6. Set a horizontal guide for your Title and one for your body text. Set vertical guides to align and size your text blocks.

Sample Page Title

Sample page body text. Lorem ipsum dolor sit amet. consect adipiscing elit. sed diem

Sample page body text. Lorem ipsum dolor sit amet. consect adipiscing elit. sed diem

7. At this point, they are just a visual aid like the grids were. Objects will not snap to them. To get that to happen, you have to click Snap to Guides.

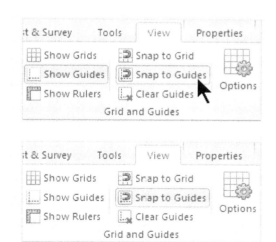

8. You can hide the Guides and still have them working. You can do this by either clicking Show Guides again or just using the keyboard shortcutd Ctrl+E to turn hide and show them.

Using the Alignment and Sizing Tools

The next set of tools are the alignment and sizing tools In the **Status** bar at the bottom of the Lectora window are the alignment tools that allow you to align objects. Note that there are several that are probably new to most of you – the centering objects on the page and making objects the same width or height.

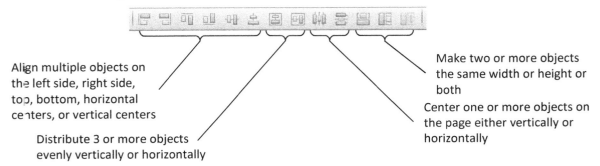

Align multiple objects on the left side, right side, top, bottom, horizontal centers, or vertical centers

Distribute 3 or more objects evenly vertically or horizontally

Make two or more objects the same width or height or both

Center one or more objects on the page either vertically or horizontally

Using Position and Size in the Status Bar

At the bottom right of your Lectora window in the status bar you will see the coordinates and size of the currently selected object. You can change any of these precisely by clicking in the box and changing the number. Clicking the green lock on the left allows you to lock the location and size of the object. This is not normally necessary but is available if you need it.

Using the Position and Size Ribbon

You can also set these properties on the **Position and Size** ribbon. The ribbon becomes available when you have selected an object by clicking on it.

You have some additional properties on this ribbon.

- **Offset:** The location of an object (x,y coordinates) are usually measured from the upper left corner of the course page. The offset properties allow you to specify that the coordinates are measured from the right and bottom of the page. This is useful when you are pasting the same objects on pages of different sizes and you want something like a Close button the same distance from the bottom on all pages.

- **Maintain Ratio:** This property allows stretch an object using any handle and it will not distort. It keeps the width and height in the same ratio – very handy for pictures.

  Remember another way to maintain the ratio is to hold the Shift key down when resizing .

- **Reset to Original:** If you have incorrectly resized an object, you can get it back to its original size by just clicking this icon.

Warning 11: Resizing some imported graphics in Lectora can *sometimes* lead to less than desirable quality. You may not see the reduced quality until the course is published. It is better to resize them in their original drawing tool and then reimport them into Lectora. If you do not have the source graphic or it is a photograph, I have found I get slightly better results by resizing it in PowerPoint® than in Lectora.

Moving Objects Around

You can move objects around in the usual ways – by dragging them or by using the arrow keys. Here are a few tips to move them *precisely* when using these methods.

- You can *constrain* movement while dragging to either vertical only or horizontal only by holding down the Shift key while dragging.

- You can move them *one* pixel at a time using the arrow keys.

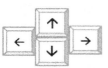

- You can move them *ten* pixels at a time using the arrow keys if you hold the Shift key down while doing so.

Refresh the Page

After moving things around and working extensively with a page, you may find that the layout is not what you expected. Before you panic, press F5 or click the Refresh icon in the Display group on the View ribbon. This will repaint the layout area as the learner will see it except for objects you have cleared the Visibility checkbox.

Find Where You Used Them

Sometimes you need to know all the places where you have used a particular resource like the ones we have covered in this step. You can locate all the pages in your course where any particular resource is used using the Resource Manager.

If you know the file name (name used in Windows® or by the Mac operating system), you can use the resource manager to find them.

1. Begin by finding one of the objects and note its file name. Go to its Properties ribbon and look in the Image box. If you can't read the entire name, click the down arrow and you may be able to there in the dropdown list. In this example, it is Condominio.gif.

2. Go to the Tools ribbon and click on the Resources icon to open the Resource Manager.

3. Click on the ⊞ next to the category of the object you are looking for. In our example, we are looking for an image.

4. Scroll down and locate the object you are looking for.

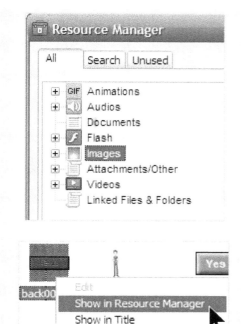

1. Another way is to click on the Title Resources tab at the right of the Lectora window. Browse around till you find the graphic you are looking for. Right click on it and select Show in Resource Manager.

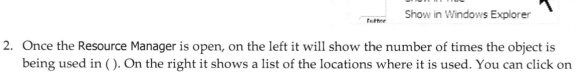

2. Once the Resource Manager is open, on the left it will show the number of times the object is being used in ( ). On the right it shows a list of the locations where it is used. You can click on any one of these lines and Lectora will take you there.

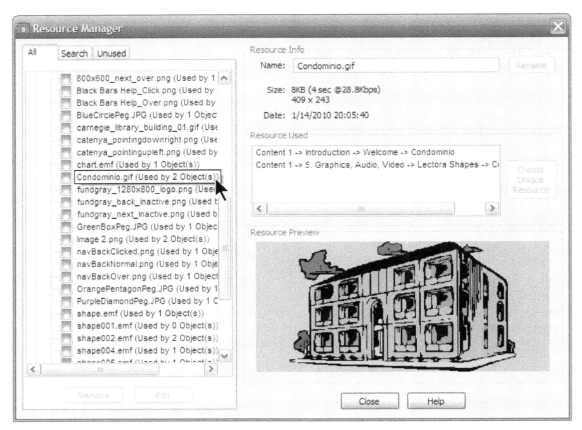

3. If you want, you can rename the object by typing in a new name in the Name box and clicking on the Rename button.

Practice What You Learned

You learned a lot about making your course more interesting in this step. Before going on, take some time to try some of these ideas on a few more pages. Experiment with different options. This way what you have learned will stay with you.

After you have done this, take a look at the file structure in Windows® Explorer. Notice any new folders that have been created and their contents.

Also, lay out a few of what you consider the typical pages in your course – some with just text, text and graphics, maybe one with an audio controller, one with a video. Then show them to your stakeholders and get their input. It is much easier to make changes now on a few pages than on your entire course later.

Remember These Key Points

- Graphics, animations, audio, and videos are easily added from the Insert ribbon and most can be edited by right clicking and selecting Edit.

- Graphics can add a lot of interest to your courses as well as improve retention.

- Graphics should be relevant to the text on the page and add to it. If they do not, then they *detract* from learning.

- Tables and charts are good ways to make facts clearer.

- Audio is best used to explain diagrams or impart emotional content.

- Animations are great for showing how things work.

- Lectora's Flash animations can help you easily make your point but beware of their limitations

- Videos are good for gaining attention, making important points, and teaching interpersonal skills.

- Use the design guidelines in this chapter to create easy-on-the-eyes professional-looking pages.

- Use the grids and guides, positioning and sizing properties, and alignment tools to arrange your page precisely.

Remember, if you want the Lectora Title that I used to create this book with **working examples**, go to www.eProficiency.com/101.html.

Step 5: Make Things Happen

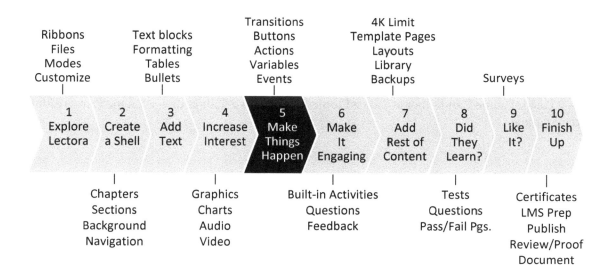

In the previous step, you have learned how to add some interest-grabbing things to your course like graphics, audio, and video. However, if anything happened, it was not really within your control; it was part of the animation or video. Now it is time to learn how to make things happen on the screen using actions and variables.

Try these ideas to making things happen.

Create Dramatic Entrances	Lectora has some nice transformations you can use when as new pages appear. You can use these to mark special pages like the first page of a topic.
Create Your Own Buttons	You can create your own buttons for the common things like navigation as well as activities.
Show and Hide Things	Everything does not have to appear as soon as the page shows. Some less important information can be shown to those who are interested by using buttons to show and hide things on the page as well as using popup windows.
Sync Bullets with Audio and Video	Yes, this is easy to do and a nice touch as long as it is not overused. As the media plays, you have bullets or graphics appear as they are discussed.
Use "Pose-able Characters	You can have a character change from one pose to another to emphasize points being made on the screen or with audio or video.
Use Hot Spots and Hyperlinks	Hot spots allow learners to click on an area on a graphic and have something appear. Hyperlinks do the same thing in text.

Another book, *Lectora 301: Techniques for Professionals*, provides extensive coverage of actions, variables, custom games, and other advanced topics which make your course even more interesting and engaging.

Use Transitions for Dramatic Entrances and Exits

Transitions produce special effects as things appear and disappear on the screen. You can control how an entire page appears using transitions at the Title, Chapter, Section, or Page level. You can control *how* individual objects or groups of objects appear and disappear.

Using *Page* Transitions

Page transitions should be used rarely as they make the page take a little longer to load and they get old quickly. The only exception is if you experience pages "flashing" as you move from one to the next when viewed in HTML. To add transitions to your page:

1. Set the default page transition on the Design ribbon. Usually this should be None.

2. Set the transition for all pages in a specific Chapter or Section by clicking on the Page Transition icon on the Chapter or Section properties.

   Set the transition for a specific Page by clicking the Page Transition icon on the Page Properties ribbon. A good place to use the Page specific transition is on the first page of each new topic to alert the learner that something is different.

3. Once you click the transition icon, Lectora opens a dialog window where you can control the kind of transition and how fast it runs.

4. Select your desired transition from the Transition dropdown list.

5. Some have their own options which you need to specify like the direction of the transition and the speed.

6. Click Run or Preview mode and try the transition out before moving on.

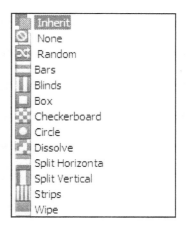

Warning 12: Page transitions may not work well over a network. If you are planning to deliver your course from a server, then be sure to try out a sample course before you have gone too far.

Using *Object* Transitions

Object transitions apply to a single object. They can apply to when the object appears as well as when it disappears. As with page transitions, use them judiciously or else they lose their impact.

1. To give an object a transition in or out, first select the object by clicking on it. Then, on its Properties ribbon, click one of the Transition buttons.

2. When you click on one of the Transition icons, Lectora opens a dialog window where you can control the kind of transition, how long before it starts, and how fast it runs.

3. The Transition dropdowns are similar to those for the page as well as the speed.

4. The delay is the amount of time *before* the transition takes place. If an object is initially Hidden, specifying a delay for Transition In does *not* make it appear after that delay. See Applying Object Transition Rules next.

Warning 13: Some objects may look a little strange when transitioning:

- In PNGs, partially transparent areas like shadows may appear black during the transition. The only known workaround is to use JPGs instead if possible.

- In PNGs, diagonal or curved lines may appear jagged during the transition. The only known workaround is to use JPGs instead if possible.

- Text blocks with a transparent background appear to have a solid white background during the transition

- In text blocks, the text may appear jagged during the transition. Compare the letters "d, q, and s" in the during and after pictures.

During Transition

diem nonu
lacreet do
volutpet. I
quis nostr
suscipit lo
This is sor

After Transition

diem nonum
lacreet dolor
volutpat. Ut
quis nostrud
suscipit lobor
This is some

Applying Object Transition Rules

Transition In happens when the object is made visible.

- If the object is initially *visible*, then the transition begins as the page appears after whatever delay is specified.

- If the object is initially *hidden*, then the transition begins when *an action on the page shows the object*. That is you must have an action somewhere such as on a button or a media event that Shows the object. Actions are covered in What Are Actions? on page 119.

Transition Out happens when a visible object is hidden either by an action or when the learner navigates to another page. The transition begins when the object is hidden after whatever delay is specified.

- If the object is *already hidden* when the learner goes to another page, transition to the next page takes place immediately.

- If the object is *still visible* when the learner goes to another page, transition to the next page takes place *after all transitions out have been completed*. For this reason, it is generally *not* a good practice to use a delay on a Transition Out unless you are sure it will have been completed by the time the learner navigates to another page. If you need to delay a transition out, use a delay on the *Hide* action we will cover later in this chapter.

 Warning 14: Transitions even with delays do *not* cause an object to appear or disappear. The delay only specifies the length of time before the transition happens. An action or navigation must trigger the showing or hiding of the object.

Warning 15: Do not use delays to sync other happenings with your audio or video because once published to HTML and run from a server/LMS, your timings could be seriously off. Use Events instead, as discussed in Getting Things to Happen on Cue While the Media Is Playing on page 141.

Use Buttons and Actions to Navigate Around the Course

Buttons are the most common way for the learner to move forward or backward in a course. While the Lectora templates come with their own buttons, most of the time you will probably be creating your own. Lectora provides ways for you to create text buttons, use some stock buttons, create transparent buttons for hot spots, and to use graphics from external sources to create buttons.

Creating buttons that do something is a two-part process. First, you have to create a graphic that will be the button. Then you have to add actions to it to make it do something.

1. Create a Graphic
- Text buttons
- Stock buttons
- Transparent buttons
- Custom buttons

2. Make It Do Something
- Attach one or more actions to the button

Part 1. Creating Graphics for Buttons

Using the button tool you can:

- create text buttons with a wizard,

- use stock buttons,

- create transparent buttons which you can use as hot spots, or

- create custom buttons where you supply all the graphics from a tool like PhotoShop® or FireWorks®.

When you have created a button, it will appear in the Title Explorer with the button icon.

As you will see later, you can really make anything into a "button" by attaching actions to it. Using a button object makes it easier to work with your course because the buttons are clearly identifiable by the icon.

 Best Practice 13: Make buttons obvious not only from the text but from the nature of the graphic. Here are two buttons, the first gives more indication that you should click on it whereas that is not so clear in the second one.

Text Buttons

Text buttons are simply buttons that say something rather than using a graphic like an arrow. They are easy to create in Lectora. The biggest advantage of Text Buttons is that you can easily change its color, size, shape, style, etc. from its properties ribbon.

1. To create a text button, select Text Button Wizard by clicking on the Button dropdown list on the Insert ribbon.

2. Select the button style from the available list.

3. In the wizard window, type in what you want the button to say and set the rest of the attributes.

   Once created, you can click on the button and access its properties. You can change pretty much anything you like there. Experiment with different settings to see what you like best.

4. Once you have clicked Finish, check it to be sure it looks right in all three states: normal, mouse over, and click. Click on the Run mode icon at the bottom of the Lectora window and try it.

One neat trick is to use a character from a symbol font like Webdings or Wingdings. You can create all kinds of symbols without using a drawing tool. Note that you *cannot* combine different fonts in one button. To access the characters in these fonts, open the Windows® Character Map available somewhere in Program Files > Accessories.

Best Practice 14: Pick a button color that allows you to:

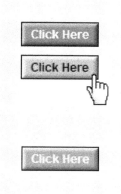

- Use a lighter color when you roll over and click like typical elevator buttons.

- Create a grayed-out version of the button for times when you want it to be disabled.

- And use a bevel to make it clear to the learner this this is a clickable button.

If you change the text in a button, you can click the resize icon to have the button automatically fit the text you have in the button.

Text buttons have several limitations. At the present time:

- You cannot combine graphics with text buttons so you can't create a button that says "Next" *and* contains a graphic (➜).

- You can only use *one* font in a given button.

If you want any of these, use the fourth option, Custom Button.

Stock Buttons

Lectora comes with a many stock buttons. When you click on the Stock Button option, Lectora opens the Stock Library. There you can select a stock button in one of several colors.

While these buttons are nice and can save some time, you cannot customize them and so there is no way to change the graphic or color. If you want a grayed-out version, you can try selecting one from the Black set.

Transparent Buttons

Use transparent buttons to create "hot spots." You might use these on top of a diagram or map and have the learner identify some part or location by clicking on it. There is an example of one coming up.

Transparent buttons appear a partially transparent blue gray in Edit mode so you can position and size them. When your course is running, they are transparent.

Custom Buttons

If you don't like any of the Lectora provided options, you can create your own using a drawing application like PhotoShop® or FireWorks®.

Custom buttons require at least one image and can have two additional ones: one for when the mouse moves over it and one when it is clicked.

You have two options:

- If you have a 3-frame animated GIF, you can use the Normal slot to specify it by clicking on the dropdown arrow, selecting one of the Browse… options, and navigating to your GIF.

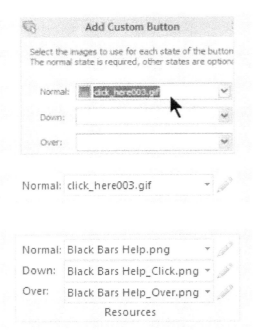

  Once you click OK, the Properties ribbon will show only one resource, the Normal state which you can change it if desired.

- If instead, you are going to supply three separate images, then click on the down arrows and navigate to where they are for each of the three states.

Warning 16: When you create the graphics for custom buttons, be sure they are all exactly the same size (same width and height in pixels) in your drawing tool. If you need to make your button a little bigger or smaller, do not resize your button in Lectora, rather resize the graphics in the source drawing tool.

Warning 17: Note that while you can create some very nice looking buttons in PowerPoint®, frequently they will *not* be the same size when saved to a file. When I do this, I copy the images to a drawing tool with a specific size canvas to make sure each image is exactly the same size and I use a resolution of 96dpi so they do not change size when imported into Lectora.

Part 2. Making It Do Something with Actions

Your buttons (except for the stock ones) do nothing once created. You must add actions to them to get them to do something.

What Are Actions?

Simply put, Lectora actions make stuff happen. An Action allows you to specify:

- **When** things happen—the event (what triggers things to happen such as when the page or object appears, when something is clicked, at a certain point in the audio, etc.)
- **What** is to happen—the action (hide, show, go to, etc.)
- The **target** of the action—whatever is to be hidden, shown, changed, where to go, etc.
- **What conditions** must be satisfied for it to happen (if xxx is true, then perform the action)
- And what **else** is to happen if the conditions are *not* satisfied

Here are a few examples:

- When a button is clicked (Trigger = On Click), show (Action) a text block (Target)
- When the Page shows (Trigger), show (Action) the next button (Target) if the question on the page has already been answered (Condition)

You can attach actions to most any object like a text block, image, a page, etc. There are some restrictions for specific actions and specific objects.

To give you an idea of the wide range of things you can do with actions, here is a table from Lectora Help file showing the possible triggers (or as they call them "events" that trigger actions), actions, and targets. Not all actions have a target and some actions have additional parts.

Trigger/On/Event	Action	Target
Any Key	Cancel Test/Survey	Chapter, Section, or Page
Hide	Change Contents	(Character/New Pose)
Keystroke	Display Message	Current Page
Mouse Click	Display Page in Popup	First Page in Title
Mouse Double-Click	Exit Title/Close Window	Last Visited Page
Mouse Enter	Flash Command	(Location in Title)
Mouse Exit	Go To	Next Chapter
Show	Go To Web Address	Next Page
Show Page	Hide	Next Section
Done Playing	Launch a program/document	(Object)
Any Key	Modify Variable	Previous Chapter
Right Mouse Click	Move	Previous Page
Timer	Mute Media	Previous Section
	None	This Object
	Open Attachment	(Tin Can Verb/Object)
	Pause	Title
	Play	Web Address
	Print Current Page	Variables
	Process Question	
	Process Test/Survey	
	Reset All Variables	
	Reset Form	
	Reset Question	
	Reset Test/Survey	
	Resize	
	Run Action Group	
	Run JavaScript	
	Send Email	
	Set Character Pose	
	Set Progress Bar Position	
	Show	
	Step Progress Bar Position	
	Stop	
	Submit Form	
	Submit Variable Values	
	Submit/Process Test/Survey	
	Tin Can Statement	
	Toggle Play Mode	
	Toggle Show/Hide	
	Unmute Media	

Using Actions to Move Around (Navigate)

When you insert a button, Lectora automatically adds a single placeholder action to it anticipating that your button will have at least one action. Sometimes buttons have more.

The default action does nothing until you change it. New actions default their trigger to Mouse Click, which means that when you click the object, the action you specified runs.

1. To change this action to do something, double-click on the action in the Title Explorer to quickly open its properties. The properties ribbon for an Action is labeled Action, not Properties.

2. In the Action and Target group, click on No Action and select the desired action from the dropdown list.

3. Once you select an action, the Action and Target group may change to provide space for other fields needed for the action. Here the target defaults to Next Page. If that is not what you want, click on the down arrow and select something else.

4. Do the same with your back button.

5. You can create buttons to go to specific **Chapters**, **Sections**, or **Pages** in your course or buttons to do other things like exit the course.

You can add an action to almost any object and make it act like a button although the icon in the **Title Explorer** will not change. Just click on the object and then click on **Action** icon ![icon] on the **Insert** ribbon or the object's **Properties** ribbon. Then customize the action as you did above.

You can easily see all the actions attached to an object and what they do by:

– first clicking on one of its actions,

– then clicking on **Action Pane** on the **Action** ribbon.

This will display the **Action Pane** below the layout area. Here you will see the name of the object to which the actions are attached and a list of the actions.

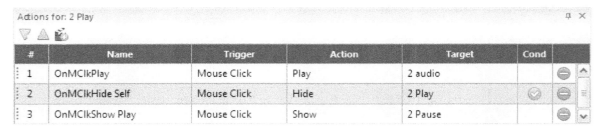

#	Name	Trigger	Action	Target	Cond	
1	OnMClkPlay	Mouse Click	Play	2 audio		⊖
2	OnMClkHide Self	Mouse Click	Hide	2 Play	✓	⊖
3	OnMClkShow Play	Mouse Click	Show	2 Pause		⊖

• If you want to add more actions, you can click on the **Add Action** icon here as well as other places on ribbons.

• You can click on any of them and make changes in the **Action** ribbon.

• You can change the order in which they run by clicking on one and then click on the green arrows to move them up to run earlier or down to run later.

• You can delete them by clicking the ⊖ on the right.

• Alternatively, you can rearrange the actions in the **Title Explorer** or delete them there.

Try It Out Before You Go Too Far

Now that you have learned a few things using transitions and actions, you should try them out before going too much further. They may not work as you expect.

Start out by trying your course in Run mode by clicking on the Run icon on the View ribbon or the smaller one at the bottom of the Lectora window. In this mode, you can no longer edit things in your course. They will behave more or less like they will in the final published version. Make sure your transitions look like you want and navigation is working.

You can also try in in Preview mode if you have a small screen. Press the Esc key to exit and return to Edit mode.

Both Run and Preview modes as well as Debug mode use the Lectora rendering engine to create the course the learner sees. There are many differences between these modes and viewing your course when it is published and viewed using a browser. Things look and behave slightly differently as well as there is no checking for errors nor do these modes use HTML, CSS, or JavaScript. You can get a free list from www.eProficiency.com/webStore and search for "differences".

Navigate Without Buttons Using Keyboard Shortcuts

Another way to navigate is by using the keyboard. You can set up most any key for the learners to use to move around to make your course more friendly to learners who prefer keyboard shortcuts to a mouse. This is how you make the PgUp and PgDn keys work like the Back and Next buttons.

1. Begin by clicking on the Title level in the Title Explorer.

2. Add an Action and select Keystroke as the action type.

3. Click in the Key box and press the desired key. Here we pressed PageDown.

4. Then in the Action and Target area make the Action Go To and the Target be the Next Page.

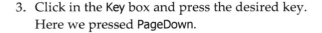

5. Repeat these steps but make the action be on keystroke PageUp and Go To the Previous Page.

Now the learner can use the Page Up and Page Down keys to move through the course as well as clicking on the navigation buttons.

Use Actions to Show and Hide Things

Let's look at how to show and hide things that on the page. Some of the reasons to do this are:

- You want the learner to click on something to show text blocks or graphics.

- You want the learner to click on a link and have a word described.

Suppose you have a graphic and you want the learner to click it to get more information.

Here's how to do it.

1. Begin by creating your text block with the description.

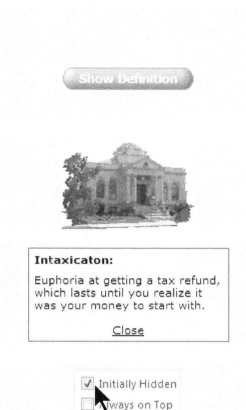

2. Check Initially Hidden property. This will hide the text block when the page is first shown.

3. Click on the graphic and add an action to it using either the Insert ribbon or the Add Object icon on the Home ribbon.

   The action will default to OnShow, which is what you want.

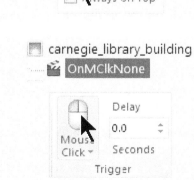

4. Click on the No Action icon in the Action and Target group and select Show.

5. The ribbon will expand so you can select a target (what you want to show). From the dropdown list, select the text block that contains the description to be shown to learners.

6. Now try it out. Click Run mode at the bottom of the Lectora window and make sure it works. The description should not be visible when you start and when you click on the graphic, the description should appear.

So far, so good. The description is now showing. If that is all you want to do, then you are done. If you want to provide a way for learners to hide the text block, here is one way.

1. Put some instructions in the text block to let learners know how to hide it. A common way is to put the word Close underlined at the bottom of the text.

2. Click on the text block and add an Action to it.

3. Change the Action to Hide and the Target to This Object.

4. Now click Run mode and try it again. You should be able to click on the graphic and have the description show. Then click on the description, which should hide it.

Control Navigation with Variables

If you stop here, the student can move forward to the next page without having to show all those things you just set up. Most of the time this is the way you should go, putting optional information on click-to-show buttons. However, sometimes you may want to force the learner to click on things before moving forward. To do that, you need to use a variable.

What Are Variables?

Wait! Don't panic. Variables are easy. They are just places in the computer memory that remember stuff or make things available to you. You can use them to keep track of things. Common examples are:

- The current page name
- The current page number
- The number of pages in the course
- The current date
- Whether the learner has clicked a button
- The number of times something has happened

All variables have a name. You can see the names of all available variables by clicking on the Variables icon in the Manage group of the Tools ribbon.

Variables have different characteristics.

- Some are automatically available and you cannot change their name. These are the ones Lectora provides for you. Some of them are shown here.

- Some are created when you create an object like a question or an entry box and you can change the name on the Properties ribbon for the object. The value of the variable is usually set by the object but it can be set with an action. For an entry box, it is what is entered by the learner, for a question , it is the answer chosen. You can change the name of these variables but you cannot delete them unless you delete the object.

- Others you create when you need the course to remember something like we need to here. You set these using a Modify Variable action.

Examples:

Variable Manager

| User-Defined | Reserved |

CurrentChapterName
CurrentDate
CurrentPageName
CurrentSectionName
CurrentTime
CurrentTitleName

Variable Manager

| User-Defined | Reserved |

Entry_0001
Entry_0002

Question_0001
Question_0002

Variable Manager

| User-Defined | Reserved |

_CourseComplete
_Fb_Data
_firstLastName
_glossary
_intaxification_shown

Using Variables to Control Navigation

While variables have many uses, let's begin by using them to control navigation. We will need to do several things.

1. Remember that the learner has clicked on the desired button or graphic.

2. Replace the Next button with one that only allows the learner to move forward under the condition that the Show button has been clicked.

1. Remember the Click

2. Adjust the Button

Let's look at exactly how to do this.

Part 1: Remember That the Button/Graphic Was Clicked

1. Add a second action to your graphic.

2. Make the action to be Modify Variable.

3. Click on the Target Property and select New Variable. If you wanted to use some other variable, you could just click on it in the list.

4. Enter the name of your variable and its initial value and click OK. If you have more than one page where you will be doing things like this, make the name unique in the course.

    –   Here we set the initial value to N meaning No, it has not been shown.

    –   We also checked the box to retain the variable between sessions in case the learner has to close the course part way through and come back another time.

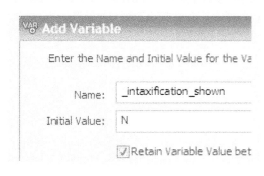

5. Then, back on the Action ribbon, in the Value property, enter a "Y" to indicate that it has been shown.

Now, when the learner clicks on the graphic to show the definition of the term, it will also run an action to set a variable to "Y" to remember that the definition has been shown.

Part 2: Adjust the Next Button

1. First, create a grayed-out version of your Next button and place it on the page.

2. Change the action to go to the next page.

3. Then, click on Always in the Conditions group and create a condition.

4. Set the condition for the learner to go to the next page.

   – Select your variable using the dropdown list in the Variable column.

   – Select Equal To in the Relationship column.

   – Enter "Y" in the Value column.

   Now your Next button will only work if the variable equals "Y".

 Warning 18: Conditions are case sensitive. This means that if you set the variable equal to a capital "Y" and then enter a lower case "y" in the Value in the Conditions, Lectora will consider them *not* equal. Be consistent; always use one case. I recommend lower case as it is one less key to press (no shift key).

You should also tell learners what the problem is if they click Next without clicking the graphic first.

5. In the Else Action group right next to the Condition group,

   click No Action and select Display Message.

6. Enter an appropriate message in the **Message** box and you are done. Now, if they click the Next button without clicking the Show button first, they will receive an instructional message.

Be sure you try this out before moving on. Start out using then Run or Preview modes.

- If things don't work right, try the **Debug** mode. It is the same as Run mode except it opens a new window that shows you all the actions as they run along with the value of the variables as they are used.

- There is a **Variables** button at the bottom of the window. Click it to see the current value of all variables available on the page. Use that window to help you solve any problems. You can also set the value of the variables there.

If what you are testing does not involve other pages (like navigation or popup windows), also try using the **Preview Page in Browser**. Sometimes things work just slightly differently in a browser.

If you cannot figure the problem out, try publishing to HTML and resolving any red errors that appear. Then try it again in **Debug** mode.

You should publish it to **Web (HTML)** from time to time to remove errors and be sure things work the same as they do in Run mode. HTML also has a **Debug** option that you can check on the HTML **Options** tab.

Naming Variables

You can name your variables pretty much anything you want. If you use an invalid character like a space or a plus sign, Lectora will tell you.

Best Practice 15: Give meaningful names to your variables. Don't use names like "X" or "Variable". When you come back in a couple of months, you may not remember what these variables are for.

Variable
_CourseComplete
_Fb_Data
_firstLastName
_glossary
_intaxification_shown

 Best Practice 16: Make the first character in all the variables *you* create an underscore "_". Why? Because it separates all your variables from all the Lectora reserved variables and it brings them to the top in the variable list. This makes it easier to find when selecting variables for actions.

In this example of a dropdown list for setting a Condition, all the user defined variables begin with "_". Notice that they are all *at the top*. If they did not begin with "_", then they would be mixed with the rest of the variables in alphabetic order. You would have to scroll every time you wanted one.

Variable
_CourseComplete
_Fb_Data
_firstLastName
_glossary
_intaxification_shown
_Lesson_Location
_mode
_temp
AICC_Core_Lesson
AICC_Core_Vendor
AICC_Course_ID
AICC_Credit
AICC_Lesson_ID
AICC_Lesson_Location

Locating Where Your Variables Are Used

On the Tools ribbon are two useful tools that can help you locate where things are used in your course: the Variable Manager and the Resource Manager. We covered the Resource Manager in the last step when we were working with objects. The other one is the Variable Manager.

The Variable Manager shows you all the places a variable is used in your course. When you click on a variable , the locations show in the Variable Used area. You can add or delete variables using the buttons at the bottom of the window. You can change the variable name, its Initial Value, and whether or not it is Retained between sessions by clicking the Edit button.

Use Actions to Create Popup Windows

Popup windows are a way for you to provide the student with optional additional information in text form or images that can explain things. The content for a popup window is *not on* the currently viewed page. Be aware that not all students will actually do whatever is necessary to open the popup window so it is a good idea to limit popups to *optional* material, *not* required material.

In Lectora, there are several actions you can use to open a popup window separate from the current page depending on what you want to do. You can simply display a text message, display another page in the course (usually smaller than the current page), open a document (sometimes called an attachment), or even go to a web page. You attach one of these actions to a button or use it somewhere to open the popup window.

Action	Usage
Display Message	Display a text message. No control over message format. OK button to close.
Display Page in Popup	Display another page in the course in a new window. Full control over format. You design close button.
Go To	Display another page in the course in a new window and specify its size and location
Open Attachment	Display a document like a PDF in a new window
Launch a Document	Open a document in its native application like MS Word®.

Displaying a Simple Text Message

Select Display Message from the dropdown list and type in your message into the Message box. You cannot format your message in any way (bold, font, size, bullets, etc.) You can click the diagonal arrow in the Message box to get a bigger window to enter your message.

When run, the message is displayed in its own window. The learner clicks an OK button to close the popup window.

Displaying Another Page in the Course

There are two ways to do this using two different actions. Before you create the popup actions, you must first create the page in your course to be shown in the popup window.

1. A good practice is to create a new Chapter at the end of your course and call it Popups. The page shown here is shown below and has the structure shown at the right. Notice that it has two ways to close the window (the X box and the Close button). The X in the Lightbox style popups is very small. Sometimes I put my own and make it red.

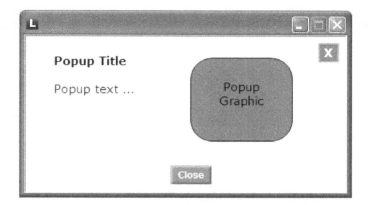

2. Now, once you have the page ready, you can add a Display Page in Popup action to your button. It shows in the Action Properties as simply Popup Page. In the Target box you select the desired page to show – here popup 1. When clicked your popup window will appear as above. You can format text and have graphics like any other page.

The Scroll To option allows you to scroll to an object on the page if you would like to position the window there. This might be handy if you had a page with glossary terms in separate text blocks.

Note that the window will have a slightly different appearance when displayed in a browser. It usually opens the window in the center of the current page and grays out the launching window (the rest of the course).

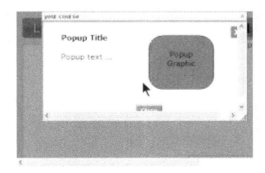

Use a "Go To" Action

You can also use a Go To action and select the page from the dropdown list.

You have the option of opening it in like the **Display Page** action or in a totally new window using the **New Window** option. If you select this option, then you can click the **New Window Properties** and set them in the dialog window shown below. Experiment to see what works best for you.

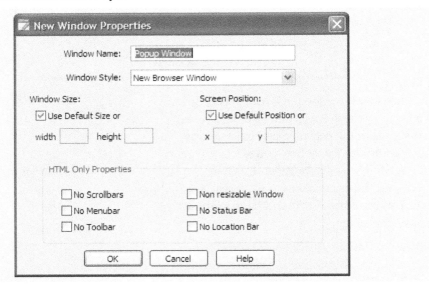

Opening an Attachment

Attachments are generally things like PDFs which most browsers support but you can have things like MS Word® documents, RTF files, etc. *as long as you are sure that the learner has the required application installed on their computer.* So, if you send someone an MS Access® file and they do not have Access® on their computer, they will not be able to open the file.

1. Create an **Open Attachment** action.

2. Then either:
    - select the desired document from the dropdown list or
    - browse for it.

When your course runs, the document will be opened in a separate window and closed by normal means using the close X box in the upper right corner of the window.

 Warning 19: Note that Lectora creates a *copy* the document and adds it to your course in the **extern** folder. If you change the original document, the copy in this folder is *not* changed. You must replace it in your **extern** folder and then republish.

Opening a Web Address

Sometimes you may want to open a web page. All you have to do is use a **Go To Web Address** action and specify the URL. You have the same options for controlling the window as you did as you do using the **Go To** action.

Make Your Audio and Video More Interactive

Audio and video are fine by themselves but you can make them interactive in a variety of ways. You already know how to put one on a page and control it with one of the many controllers. Many times that is enough but sometimes you don't want the controller because it allows the learner to skip forward. So, you eliminate the controller but best practice is to allow the learner to pause, restart, and replay the media. In addition, you may want things to show up at certain points while the media is playing. This is what we cover here.

Creating Your Own Play and Pause Buttons

You can create your own buttons to have actions to Play, Pause, Stop, Mute, and Unmute the media.

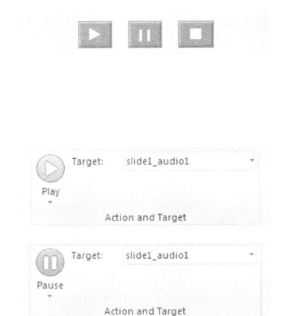

1. First, create three buttons for your actions, one to play, one to pause, and one to stop the media. These buttons are made using the Text Button wizard in Lectora. The play and stop buttons shown here were made using a Wingding font and the pause was 2 I's with a space between them.

2. Click on the Play button and add a Play action.

3. Click on the Pause button and add a Pause action.

Now you have the basics. But normally only the Play or Pause button shows and the other is hidden. So, here is what we do. We add a couple of actions to each button to hide itself and show the other button.

4. Click on the Play button and an action to hide itself.

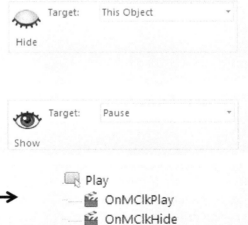

5. Add another to Show the Pause button. Your

Now the Play button should look something like this in the Title Explorer or like the below in the Action Pane.

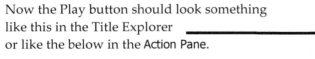

Actions for: 2 Play

#	Name	Trigger	Action	Target	Cond	
1	OnMClkPlay	Mouse Click	Play	2 audio		⊖
2	OnMClkHide Self	Mouse Click	Hide	2 Play	✓	⊖
3	OnMClkShow Play	Mouse Click	Show	2 Pause		⊖

6. Do something similar on the Pause button. Add actions to hide itself and show the Play button. It should look like this.

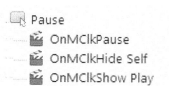

Best Practice 17: Normally the Play and Pause buttons are one on top of the other so that you only see one at a time. However, when you are testing something, it is best to have them only *partially overlap* so you can see clearly what is happening.

Check the Initially Hidden property of the Play button. When you run your course, the audio should start automatically. When learners click the Pause button, it will pause the media, hide itself, and show the Play button. When they click the Play button it will resume the audio, hide itself, and show the Pause button.

1. Now on to the Stop button. Add an action to stop the media.

2. You also need to add a couple of actions so the learner can start playing it again. Copy the Hide Self and the Show Play actions from the Pause button and paste on the Stop button.

3. Click on the Hide Self action and change it so it hides the Pause button.

4. Do something similar for the Play action.

5. Change its name to say Hide Pause. Now when you click the Stop button, it not only stops the media but also hides the Pause button and shows the Play button enabling the learner to restart the media.

In the above examples, I changed the names of the actions in the Title Explorer to be more descriptive. In earlier versions of Lectora, this made it much easier to understand quickly what was going on. Beginning with Lectora 11, the Action Pane now shows even more information, is easier to read, and is much more reliable.

Mute & Unmute

There are two other actions you can use on buttons. They apply to all media that is playing audio. The audio continues to play but you cannot hear it. I cannot figure out when I would use these as I would not want the learner to miss any of the material.

Getting Things to Happen When the Media Is Done Playing

While the audio is playing, the Pause button is showing so learners can pause it if they want. When it gets to the end, the Pause button is still showing and there is no way for the student to replay the audio short of going to another page and coming back. So, at the end of the audio we need to have the Play button showing, *not* the Pause.

All audio and video types allow you to have one or more actions that take place at the *end* of the media using Done Playing action. We will use this to fix our problem. We will put a couple of actions on the audio controller that hide the Pause button and show the play button at the end of the audio.

1. Copy the hide and the show actions from the Stop button. One of these hides the Pause button and the other shows the Play button.

2 Click on the audio controller and paste.

3. Click on the Hide Pause action and change it so that its trigger is Done Playing.

4. It is also good practice to change the name so that it accurately describes what the action now does – change OnMClk to OnDone.

5. Change the Show Play action from Mouse Click to Done Playing.

6. Change its name from OnMClk to OnDone.

You can put other actions on the media as well. Probably the most common one is to hide the Next button until the media is finished playing and then show it. If you do that, you should use some advanced techniques to remember *not* to force the student to listen to the media after the first time on the page by using variables.

Getting Things to Happen on Cue While the Media Is Playing

Now you know how to get something to happen when it is finished playing, but how about *while* it is playing? MP3 and FLV file types allow you to have things happen *while* the audio is playing as well. If you have another file type, Lectora provides the means to convert it as we covered in Converting Audio on page 90. Getting things to happen is a two-part process.

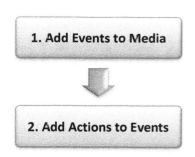

First, you have to add events (sometimes called "cue points" or "trigger points") to the media using the appropriate media editor. Then in Lectora, you add actions on the events.

Add Events

1. There are several ways to do this. You can right click on the object and select Edit, click the Edit icon on its Properties ribbon, or probably the easiest is to click on the Sync Events icon in the Playback Options group on its Properties ribbon. This will open the Synchronize Events dialog box.

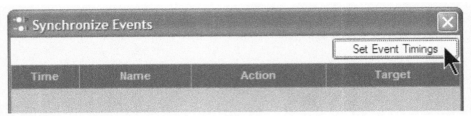

2. Click on the Set Event Timings button to open the media editor.

   When the media editor opens, you will see the media and a timeline.

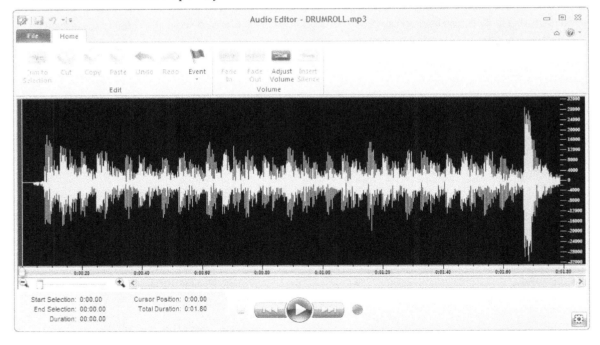

3. Play the media to the point where you want something to happen. Click Pause.

4. Click the Event icon in the media editor's Home ribbon.

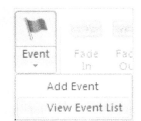

5. The Event dialog window will open to confirm your event. Click OK. A red arrow will appear on the timeline where the event is.

6. Continue this process until you have all the events you want.

7. If you want to change the time of an event or delete it, click on the Event icon and select Event List from the dropdown list.

   When the Event List opens, you can click on an event and then change the time or name or remove it.

8. Save your changes and close the editor.

 Warning 20: If you decide to change the names of the events from the default "Event n", be sure you use *unique* names within the file. Sometimes there is a problem if two events have the same name. If you have more than one audio or video file, make sure the names *are not duplicated* between them.

Add Actions to Events

Now the Synchronize Events dialog window should look something like this with the events showing but nothing happening (no actions).

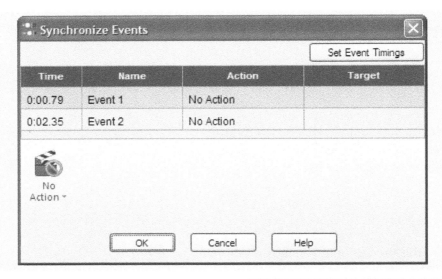

9. Click on an event to select it and then click the action icon in the lower part of the window. Initially they are all set to No Action.

10. Select your action and set the rest of the parameters for that action as needed. In the example shown here, we show the first bullet at 1.72 seconds into the media and the second bullet at 2.98 seconds.

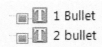

In this example, 1 Bullet and 2 Bullet are separate text blocks on the page.

| 1 Bullet |
| 2 bullet |

Using Groups of <u>Objects</u> to Show More

If you want to show more than one object on an Event, just put them in something called a Group. Groups very much like the groups you have in PowerPoint®. When objects are grouped, if you move one, you move them all. You can show and hide the entire group or individual objects can be shown or hidden. Suppose you wanted to show the text for the first bullet along with a graphic. Here is what you would do.

1. Select both the bullet text block and the graphic by holding down the Ctrl key and clicking on each object.

2. Then right click on one of them and select Group

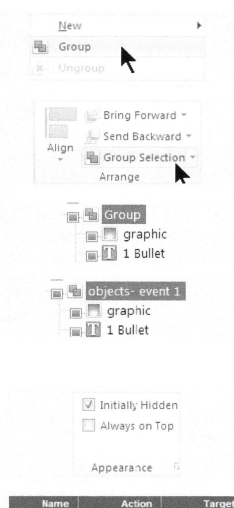

or click on Group Selection in the Arrange group on the Home ribbon.

3. Lectora will create a group and put both objects in it. In the Title Explorer, can drag other objects into it if you want or drag the ones in there out.

4. Rename the group to something meaningful. Since there will be other kinds of groups, a good practice is to begin the name with the word "objects-" because there are other kinds of groups that can contain actions.

5. In the Group's Properties, check the Initially Hidden property so these do not show when the page is first presented.

6. Now change the Target of the action for the first event to be this group. When it runs, it will show all the objects in the group.

A Couple of Quick Notes about Groups

- If you want to add objects to an existing group, you can drag them into the group in the Title Explorer. This does *not* work on the page layout area.

- Once you have objects in a group, they all move together, even if you just drag one of them. If you want to move *just one* of them, hold the Alt key down while moving the desired object with the mouse or the arrow keys.

- You can ungroup objects by right clicking on the ones you want to ungroup or the whole group in the Title Explorer and then

  - selecting Ungroup from either the right-click menu or from the Home ribbon or

  - just dragging them out of the group in the Title Explorer.

- Groups may not contain other groups like you can do in PowerPoint®.

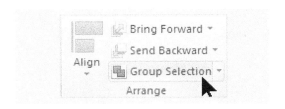

Using Groups of <u>Actions</u> to Do More

Now suppose when you show the second bullet, you want the text for the first bullet to stay on the screen but you want the graphic to be go away. Remember, you can only have one action on the event. While there are several ways to do this, probably the cleanest way is to create a *group* of actions rather than objects. Here's how.

1. Start by inserting a Group from the Insert ribbon.

2. Immediately, while it is selected, click on the Action icon to add an action.

3. Make this action Show the second bullet like we did before on the event.

4. Click Add Action to add a second action.

5. Make this second action hide the graphic that belonged to the first bullet.

6. Change the names of the actions to clearly describe what they do.

7. Change the Group's name to something meaningful and indicate the it is an action group.

8. Now click on the media file again and on the Sync Events icon in its properties. Click on the action icon in the Synchronize Events dialog window and select Run Action Group and make the action group your Target.

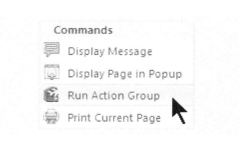

When you are done, your Events window should look something like this.

Now when the media reaches the second event it will run the action group which consists of showing the second bullet and hiding the first graphic.

Name	Action	Target
Event 1	Show	objects- event 1
Event 2	Run Action Group	actions- event 2

Use "Pose-able" Characters to Make Your Point

Lectora now provides a whole host of characters with some 15 different poses each. These can be used as simple avatars. They have the following poses:

1. Arms crossed
2. Happy
3. OK Sign
4. Pointing down left
5. Pointing down right
6. Pointing middle left
7. Pointing middle right
8. Pointing up left
9. Pointing up right
10. Sad
11. Thinking
12. Thumbs Down
13. Thumbs Up
14. Waving
15. Writing

You can change the pose using a Set Character Pose action. Like any other special effect, be careful not to over use it.

1. Click on the Character icon on the Insert ribbon.

2. This will open the Stock Library. Browse around and find an appropriate character.

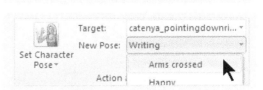

3. Then when you need to change the pose, use a Set Character Pose action.

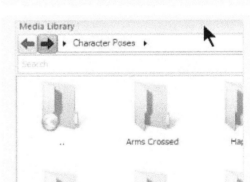

If you don't find characters you want, you can actually do this yourself using a Change Contents action although it just a bit more trouble. This technique works not just with characters, but also with any set of images where you want to replace one with the other.

1. Put your first image on the page where you want it.

2. Add a Change Contents action to the desired button.

3. Then in the Target dropdown list, select the object that you want to be replaced.

4. In the Resource dropdown list select the one you want to replace it with. If you don't see it, you can browse for it using one of the options available.

 Warning 21: When you use this technique, be sure that all the images are exactly the same size in pixels when you start. And, as always, set that size in a drawing tool. If you do not, the replacements may appear grainy or pixelated.

Use Hot Spots

Hot spots are useful when you want to have the learner move their mouse over things and have things appear and disappear. You have already learned about transparent buttons. At the time, you learned to put On Click actions on them. Here we will use On Enter and On Exit actions to show a graphic when the mouse is moved over the button and hide it when the mouse is moved off it.

Suppose you have a diagram and you want to show descriptive text when the learner moves their mouse over part of the diagram. Follow these steps.

1. Have the object (here a text block) you want to show and hide not visible when the page appears by checking the Initially Hidden property.

2. Create a transparent button using the Button icon on the Insert ribbon.

3. Place it where you want it. Here we put it on top of the first step in the diagram.

4. Change the trigger for the action that comes with the button to Mouse Enter.

5. Change the Action and Target to Show the object.

6. Add another action to the transparent button to hide the object when the mouse leaves using the Mouse Exit trigger.

7. Now click on the Run mode button and try it out. When the mouse moves over the transparent button, it should turn to a hand and the description should show.

Use Hyperlinks for More Info

Hyperlinks typically are words within text that are clickable and bring up a popup of some kind. Probably the most common use is for terms where the learner can click on the term and bring up a definition. You can also show objects on the same page or many other things. Let's see how to bring up a popup page with a word from the glossary.

First, decide what kind of popup you want to use and create it we described in Use Actions to Create Popup Windows on page 133.

1. Select the text you want to make a hyperlink and then either click the Hyperlink icon on the Home ribbon or right click and select Add Hyperlink from the dropdown list.

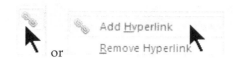

2. This will open up the Hyperlink dialog window where you set the action to do what you want it to do.

3. You can change the hyperlink at any time by double clicking on it to reopen the dialog window.

4. You can remove the hyperlink by clicking inside the text and then right clicking and selecting Remove Hyperlink.

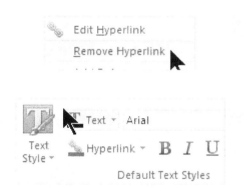

5. If you want to change the color of the hyperlink throughout your course, click on the Hyperlink icon on the Design ribbon and select your color.

Practice What You Learned

Best Practice 18: Any time you create something you have never tried before or even the first time in this course, you should make sure it works by clicking on Run or Preview mode and trying it before you leave the page. Then try it in HTML just to be sure.

You learned a lot about making things happen in this step. Before going on, take some time to create a few more pages and apply these techniques. Experiment with different options. This way what you have learned will stay with you.

If you are going to be using any particular technique many times in your course, run it by some of your stakeholders after you have a couple of typical ones done and *before* you have a lot of them done to be sure everyone is on board with the way things work.

Remember These Key Points

In this step, you learned how to take a course made up of static content and make it more active and interesting by making things happen on the screen either by themselves or by having the learner click on something. You learned to:

- Use transitions for more dramatic entrances and exits or to signal an important page.

- Use buttons with actions to move around the course or hide and show things.

- Have things appear and disappear as your audio or video play.

- Use "pose-able" characters to liven things up a bit.

- Create shortcut keys to make the course more friendly for some users.

- Use hot spots and hyperlinks to show additional detail.

- Remember to make required content show automatically and optional content appear when a button or link is clicked.

- Just a note before we get started. If you want the Lectora Title that I used to create this book with

Step 6: Make Your Course Engaging

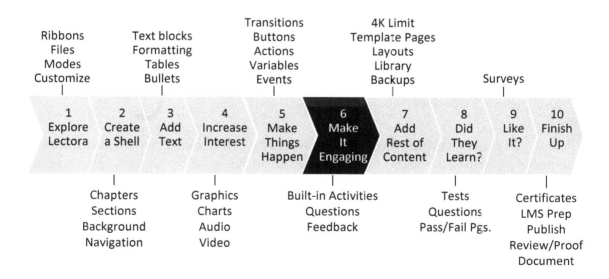

You just learned how to make your course interesting—to hold the learners' attention. However, they really did not have to *do* much other than click on this or mouse over that. There is a big difference between interesting and engaging. Interesting is like watching a good movie. Engaging on the other hand requires you participate and really think.

In this step, we will draw the learner more and more into the course and increase the effectiveness of the course by:

Adding Built-in Activities	Lectora comes with some built in activities that make it easy to add games to your course. These will draw learners in but they have several drawbacks.
Create Exercises	Exercises are simply questions that apply the content to a situation and have the learner decide what to do. You don't just drop in a question. You need to construct good feedback, possibly restrict the number of attempts and forward navigation as well as what happens if learners return to the page.

So far, learners are still pretty much working in a passive mode. Information is being pushed into their brain but they have not had to use it. All you have really done is to get them *familiar* with the material. The likelihood that they can tell someone what they learned or use the material is relatively low.

Now it is time to learn how to make your courses more thought-provoking and truly engaging. Research has shown that most students learn more when they have to use/apply what they are learning. This process causes the brain to strengthen the neural pathways that retain the new information.

To do this, you present a situation to the learner where the new information is applied and ask a question. Simply getting the learner to recall the information is *not* sufficient although it is better than nothing. The material needs to be *applied* by the learner to a life-like situation. Here are a few model questions:

- "You walk into the office/shop/lab... and see ... What would you do? Or, what would you recommend that person do?"

- Drag the process steps into the proper order.

Some tips:

- Create a job-related setting for the question so the student is applying the material to a job/task and not to some sort of unrelated game.

- Avoid True/False questions as they are too easy and do not require enough thinking.

- Use drag and drop rather than matching as the matching crisscrossed lines do not enhance memory.

- Avoid "all of the above" and "none of the above" answer choices as they are confusing.

- When the learner answers the question, give meaningful real-world feedback and possibly explain why it was wrong.

If you don't use exercises like these, you should save yourself a lot of time and money and just create a PDF. To make an e-learning course worthwhile, you need to engage the learner by having them *apply the content*. Let's look at how to do this.

Use Lectora's Built-in Activities

The built-in activities are simply Flash® animations.

1. Begin by selecting a Flash Activity from the Flash dropdown list on the Insert ribbon.

1. This will open the Flash Activities portion of the Stock Library. Select one of the many games that are available – bowling, basketball, car race, categories, dunking booth, etc.

2. That will open a wizard window where you specify the many options for the activity. When you are done, you can see how it looks by clicking the Run mode button at the bottom of the screen.

3. You can change the choices you made by clicking on the Flash Parameters on its Properties ribbon.

4. If you want to restrict movement until the game is over, you can use an OnDonePlaying action the same way we did for audio and video.

Warning 22: While easy to set up, these activities do have several limitations, some of which we have already mentioned.

- You are relatively limited in your feedback to something like "Correct" or "Incorrect" in many of these activities. Best practice is to give the learner an explanation *why* the answer selected is wrong.

- The settings for the activities are *not* work related. Rarely do people play tic tac toe or Jeopardy as part of their job. For maximum transfer to work, the game should be related to the job.

- It can be difficult to show the correct answer when there are more than 2 choices.

- Many of the activities are limited to two choice answers, which does not really challenge the learner and give them an opportunity to apply what they are learning.

- Spell check does not check the text.

Add Exercises Using Questions

Questions are a great way to help the learner master the material. Question objects can appear in a test or *anywhere in your content*. That is, questions are *not* limited to a test.

When you design questions in Lectora, you have several things to consider:

- What is the question and the answer choices (correct answer and distractors)?

- What will be the feedback and when is it given?

- Is there a limit to the number of attempts?

- What happens if the learner returns to the page?

Inserting a Question

Let's begin by inserting a simple question. Then we will move on to giving feedback and limiting the attempts.

1. On the **Test & Survey** ribbon, click on the **Ques-**
   tion icon. You can select the question type from
   the dropdown list there or change it clicking
   on the same icon in the **Question Creator**.

   Once clicked, Lectora opens the **Question Crea-**
   tor (wizard).

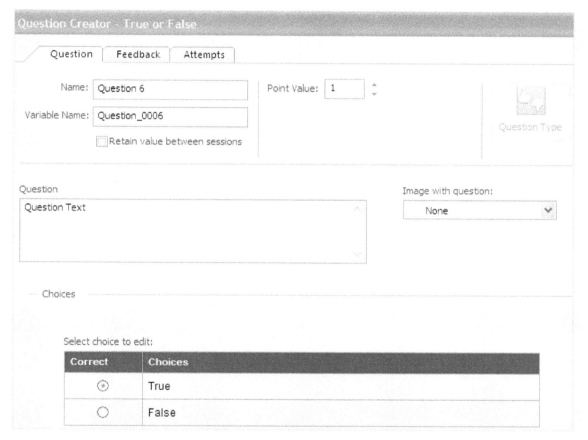

2. In the top area, you don't need to do much.
   - If you anticipate that learners will revisit the course and you want to show what they an-
     swered last time, then check the **Retain value between sessions**. In most instances you are lim-
     ited to 4000 characters of retained information for an *entire course* so be careful how you
     use this.
   - The **Point Value** is used for tests and is covered later.
   - You can change the question type by clicking on the **Question Type** icon and selecting from
     the list.

Warning 23: Once you have clicked OK on the question wizard, you can no longer change the question type. You can switch Multiple Choice to Multiple Response questions but that seems to be about all.

3. In the middle area, click in the Question box and enter your question. You cannot format the text now, but you can change it in its text block after you have closed the Question Creator.

4. If you have an image you want associated with the question, select it using the dropdown box

5. The bottom area changes depending on the type of question you have selected. Here you indicate the correct choice(s) and specify the text and/or graphics for the choices. Let's look briefly at the common properties and then a little each type.

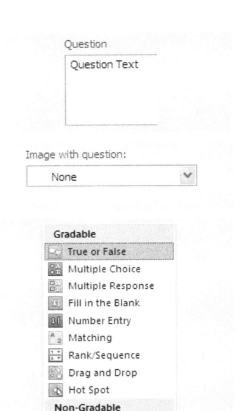

Choice Properties Common to Most Questions

Most questions have the following things in common in the Choices area.

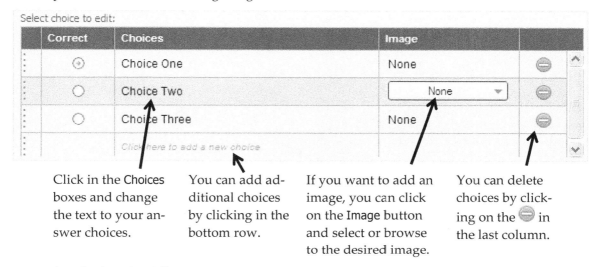

Click in the Choices boxes and change the text to your answer choices.

You can add additional choices by clicking in the bottom row.

If you want to add an image, you can click on the Image button and select or browse to the desired image.

You can delete choices by clicking on the ⊖ in the last column.

Let's take a look at the different question types and their options.

True or False Questions

True/False questions are some of the *weakest* questions you can use from an instructional design standpoint. Multiple Choice questions with 4 or more choices are much better.

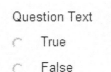

Question Text

   ○ True

   ○ False

In the Choices area:

  a. Indicate the correct answer by clicking the appropriate radio button Correct column.

  b. If desired, you can click in either of the choices boxes and change the text, Yes and No for example.

Multiple Choice Questions

We are all familiar with Multiple Choice questions that look like this.

Question Text

   ○   Choice One

   ○   Choice Two

   ○   Choice Three

In addition to the common presentation above, you can elect to have the choices shown in a dropdown list where learners select their choice from a list by clicking on the down arrow and clicking on a choice.

Question Text

	⌄

Choice One
Choice Two
Choice Three

In the Choices area:

a. If you want the answer choices reordered each time the learner visits the page, check the Randomize choices box*.

b. Indicate the correct answer by clicking the appropriate radio button in the Correct column.

c. If you want the answer choices listed in a dropdown list instead of all being shown at once on the page, check the Show choices as droplist box.

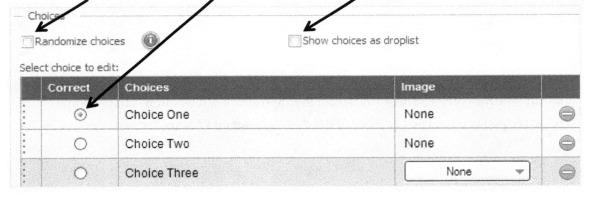

*If you randomize, note that you need to make sure that the text blocks should be big enough to hold *any* answer.

Multiple Response Questions

Multiple Response questions are simply multiple-choice questions where you must click more than one choice. Typical questions end with "Check all that apply." Learners see check boxes instead of radio buttons.

Question Text... Check all that apply.

   ☐   Choice One

   ☐   Choice Two

   ☐   Choice Three

When you create Multiple Response questions, check all the correct choices in the Correct column. The learner must check *all* the checked answers for the question to be considered correct.

Fill in the Blank Questions

Fill in the Blank questions are just that.

Complete the following statement: A ... is called a [   ]

Enter your answer in the box above.

Fill in the blank questions give you some new choices.

a. If you want the learner to enter one of the correct choices *exactly* including extra spaces and punctuation select ANY answer . If you simply want all the choices to be present in the answer regardless of punctuation or surrounding letters, select All answers. For example, if the correct answer is aaa then ANY requires aaa and only aaa to be correct while ALL considers bAaac to be correct.

b. If you want the learner to be able to press the enter key and enter multiple lines, check the Multi-Line box.

c. Turn on Case Sensitive if that matters.

d. Set the Text Limit to as near as you can to the entry length.

Number Entry Questions

Number Entry questions are a special form of the Fill in the Blank question. They are good when you want to allow the entry of numeric answers that must fall within certain criteria. You specify the rules the number must satisfy to be considered correct. You can require that the answer satisfy any one of the rules or all of the rules.

Question Text

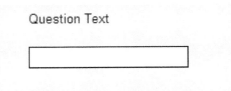

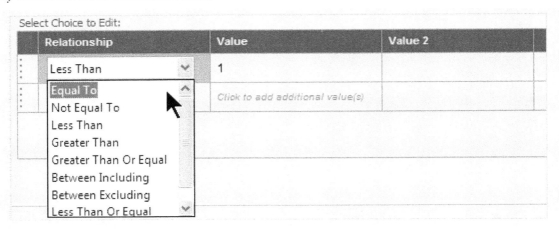

Matching Questions

Matching questions now offer more capabilities than previous versions in Lectora. You specify not only the text and optional image that is to appear in the matching pairs, but you can now specify the names that will appear in the answer variable and the color and width of the lines. The Names default to 1, 2, 3, … but you can change them to anything you want.

Question Text

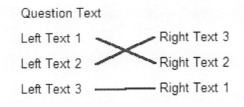

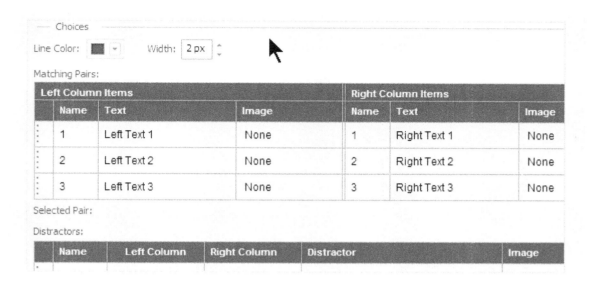

 Best Practice 19: While matching questions sound nice and are quite common, they do not help the learner remember the material. The answer is a bunch of crisscrossed lines connecting things. If you can, it is much better to *use a drag and drop question* so that when done, the page is something that you want the learner to remember.

Rank/Sequence Questions

The Rank/Sequence question gives the learners a list of choices and has them indicate the proper order by selecting options from dropdown list as shown here. Again, a drag and drop is a better choice than *this* form of the Rank/Sequence question because drag and drop shows the objects in the proper sequence and this is what you want the learner to remember.

However, if you check the Show Choices In Droplist, your question is much more memorable. The correct answer *does* show the objects in the proper sequence.

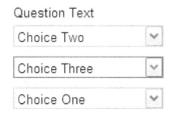

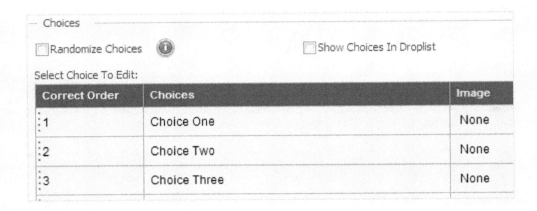

Drag and Drop Questions

Drag and Drop questions have the learner drag items to the proper location. They are good choice when teaching concepts that involve things being in a certain order or belonging to a certain category.

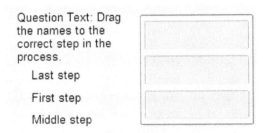

The drag and drop question has many options.

a. As with the matching question, you can now give text names to the answers that will appear in the answers shown on the Results pages in a test.

b. If you specify an image, then the image is the draggable item; the associated text will not move when run.

c. Each Drag item may have one or more correct drop zones. This allows you to have multiple items dropped in any order into any number of correct locations. For example, you could have two bowls for drop zones and several different fruits and vegetables. The learner would drag the fruits to one bowl and the vegetables to the other.

d. Drop zones are independent of the drag items. You can make them any size you want and position them precisely by clicking on the ⬚ icon on the right (not shown).

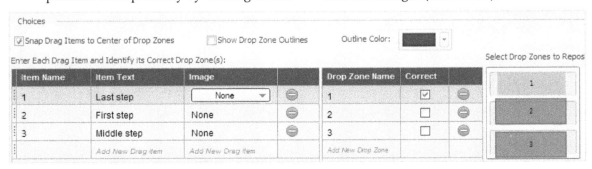

Hot Spot Questions

Hot Spot questions have learners click on desired locations.

The big improvement in the hot spot question from previous versions of Lectora is that now, instead of just radio buttons, you can have rectangular transparent areas like transparent buttons.

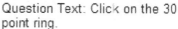

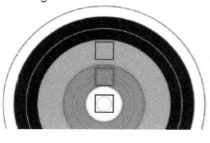

Hot Spot Image: (Required)

TrivSampleHotSpotImage.p

Hotspot

Transparent Area

Radio Button/Check Box

Transparent Area

In the question properties you specify the image that will have the hot spots and the kind of hot spots you want.

You can make the hot spots any size you want and position them precisely by clicking on the icon on the right in the Choices area.

Short Answer Questions and Essay Questions

Short answer and essay questions are not gradable. There are no correct choices nor is there any way to check the response for key words other than by using JavaScript, a very advanced technique. They are simply an entry box where the learner can enter some text and get general feedback. For example, "Enter in the box below what you think the supervisor should do." The feedback would then give the recommended course of action.

Question Text... Enter your answer in the box below.

Likert Questions

Likert questions are questions where the learner ranks their opinion on one or more items along a scale. There is no feedback for this question type nor is it gradable.

In the Question Creator, click on each statement and change the text to what you want.

	Agree	Neither Agree nor Disagree	Disagre
Statement One	●	●	●
Statement Two	●	●	●
Statement Three	●	●	●

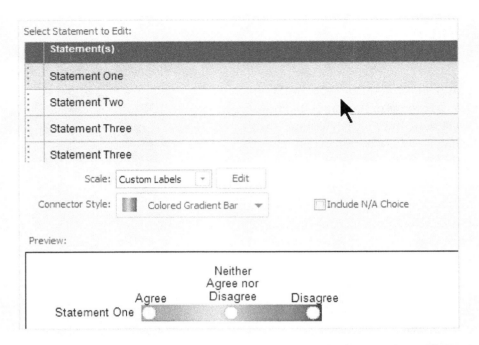

Select the scale from a list of predefined scales or design your own using the **Custom Labels** option.

Set the **Number of Choices**. Note that once you click OK and you exit the **Question Creator**, you cannot change the number of questions in the list. So, if you are unsure, create a few extra.

Select the **Connector Style** in the dropdown list.

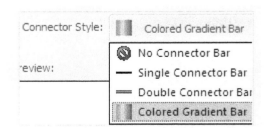

Additional Notes

- Once you have clicked OK in the question wizard and closed the window, you can still edit the question but you cannot change the question type other than switching between Multiple Choice and Multiple Response.

- You can format the text in any of the text blocks (question, answer choices) like any other text block. You do not have to open the Question Creator.

Giving Feedback.

Giving feedback on questions includes:

- *what* you are going to give (text, graphics, etc. i.e. its content) as well as
- *when* feedback appears.

What Feedback You Give (Content)

Giving feedback is an important part of the questions. Simple positive feedback like "Correct" is fine but simple negative feedback like "Incorrect" is not. If you are serious about the student learning something, they need to be given feedback that tells them what the consequences of making that choice would be and why it is incorrect. Here is an example.

Question: A customer walks in and asks … Which of the below would be the best choice?"

Feedback for choice 1: "The customer frowns and walks out. When a customer asks a question …"

Feedback for choice 2: "The customer smiles and asks another question. …"

In this book, we will cover the feedback options included with the Lectora questions. *Lectora 301: Techniques for Professionals* covers techniques to give even more customized feedback. *Designing Effective eLearning* gives you many more ideas for feedback.

1. To provide feedback, begin by clicking on the Feedback tab in the Question Creator and check Enable Feedback. If you have already closed the Question Creator you can open it easily by clicking on Edit Feedback on the Question Properties ribbon.

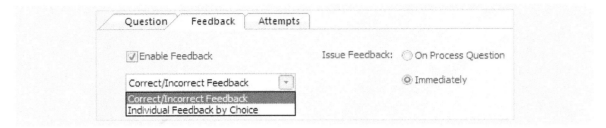

The Issue Feedback Property is covered in the next topic on When Feedback Appears on page 169.

2. For some questions like multiple-choice and multiple response, you can give different feedback for each answer choice. This is a good idea as it gives you a chance to give students more precise explanation as to why their choice was not the best one.

3. Once you have enabled feedback, the lower part of the Feedback page changes to allow you to create the kind of feedback you want. You click on one of the rows and it changes color to indicate that it is selected. Below these rows is an area where you can specify one action that will provide feedback. Normally this is Display Message.

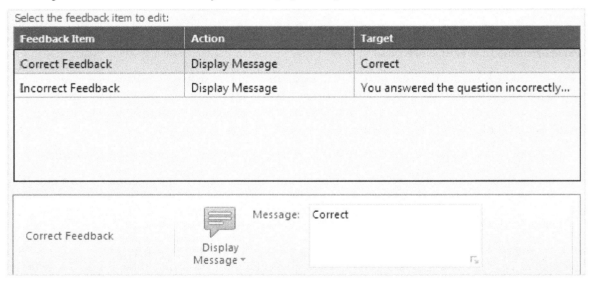

If you have more than one thing to do you can put the actions in a group and use a Run Action Group action (see Using Groups of Actions to Do More on page 146).

 Warning 24: As of April, 2013, the text in the Display Message action in a question is *not* checked by the spell checker. For that reason alone it is better to use hidden text blocks for correct and incorrect feedback *on the page* that are shown as needed.

When Feedback Appears

There are three times when feedback can naturally appear:

- Immediately when the an answer choice is selected

- When a Process Question action is run (usually when a button is clicked)

- When the learner leaves the page by clicking a navigation button

While **Immediately** works fine for true/false and multiple-choice, it can surprise learners on other types of questions. For example, on drag and drop and matching questions, it does not appear until the items have been moved or matched.

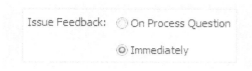

In multiple response questions, it appears when learners have checked the number of items equal to the number of correct items. That is, it does not appear as soon as learners select an incorrect choice. Therefore, if you want learners to check three out of five choices, nothing happens when they have checked just two; they must check three for immediate feedback to occur.

If you check **On Process Question**, feedback takes place either when a Process Question action is run or when the learner leaves the page, whichever comes first.

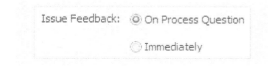

No Button

If you do not have a button on the page to process the question, then when learners click Next, they receive whatever feedback you specified.

- If you used a Display Message, then the message will appear and learners *may* have to click OK before they can advance. *Be sure to try this option out when published to HTML or and LMS.*

- If you chose to show something on the page, the learner *will not see it* as the Next button has already taken them to the next page.

Button

One common practice is to create a button with a Process Question action on it. Some people use "Submit" on the button but I prefer something like "Check Answer." Then, when learners are satisfied with their choices, they click the button to receive feedback.

Check My Answer

Best Practice 20: When deciding what feedback to give and when to give it:

- Be consistent – use the same type and timing on all exercises if possible. Avoid popup windows on some while on others you show text blocks on the page. Avoid immediate feedback on some while on others you use a Check Answer button.

- Create several versions and have a couple of people try them to see how well they work. Pick the one that is the most user friendly.

- Use On Process Question in tests as it gives learners a chance to change their mind.

Restricting the Number of Attempts

Generally, it is a good idea to let learners try several times before giving them the correct answer. However, be careful not to frustrate the student by making the question too hard to answer correctly. For example a simple multiple response question (check all that apply) with four choices has 15 different possible answer combinations. At some point, usually after two or three tries, it is a good idea to give the learner a hint or even the correct answer.

In this book, we will cover using the Attempts tab to limit the number of tries and then provide the correct answer. For ways to count the number of tries, see *Lectora 301: Techniques for Professionals*.

On the Question Properties ribbon, you can easily see if feedback in enabled and how many attempts are allowed.

If you click the Edit Attempts icon, it opens the Attempts tab of the Question Creator.

You can simply lock the question after the maximum attempts or you can lock it *and* give some feedback too.

Restricting Forward Navigation Until Question Is Answered

Some learning situations require that learners answer questions or complete exercises before moving forward. As we did with audio and video, you need to disable the Next (Forward) button and then enable it when the question is answered. (Note that Test Chapters provide a much easier way to do this. You can put all your content in a Test Chapter and exclude the Test from the overall score.)

For Immediate Feedback

1. First, create a grayed-out Next button and place it in front of the active Next button on the exercise page. It should have an action on it that tells learners that they must answer the question before moving on.

2. Create a Group for your correct feedback actions and another for your incorrect feedback.

3. Add an action to give feedback to each group using the Display or Show actions we covered in Step 5: Make Things Happen.

4. Add a Hide action to hide the grayed-out Next button.

5. On the Feedback panel of the Question Properties, run the appropriate group for correct and incorrect feedback items.

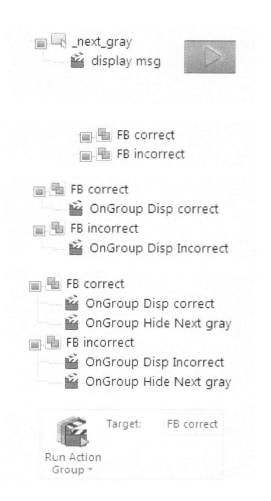

For Feedback Using a Button

If you are using a button like Check Answer to give feedback, you need to take a slightly different approach.

The first thing to know that Lectora stores the answers learners select in a variable. Remember that a variable is just a named place in computer memory. If you have a True/False question, the variable contains either "True" or "False". If you have a multiple-choice question, it contains the text you entered in the question wizard for the answer choice selected. Until the learner selects an answer choice, the question variable is empty.

1. Begin by going to the Question Properties and noting the *name* of the Variable for the question.

2. On your Check Answer button, add an action to give correct feedback.

3. On the Properties ribbon for the correct feedback action, click on the Always icon in the Conditions group.

4. In the pane that opens, select the question variable and Is Correct for a Relationship.

5. Once you click OK, a new group will appear in the Action Properties – the Else Action. This action runs if the condition is *not* true, i.e. the question is *not* correct. So click on it and select the desired action to run just like you did for the correct action.

6. Now add one more action to hide the grayed-out Next button.

7. Set its condition to run if the question variable is not empty – i.e. the learner has at least tried to answer the question. This way you prevent the learner from just clicking the Check Answer button to move on. They have to at least try once.

Crafting a Revisited Page

Next, you should consider what happens if learners return to the exercise page. If they answered it incorrectly, what will show? You have a couple of choices. You can:

- Do nothing in which case the last answer selected will appear. If it is wrong, the learner may falsely interpret it as the correct answer since there is no feedback indicating otherwise.

- Display the correct answer (which is not easy in most cases).

- Clear the question if it was incorrect and force the learner to retry the question.

- Show the feedback if the answer is not correct. This works best if the feedback is in a text block on the page because if you use something like a Display Message action, it is a little odd to land on a page and immediately have a message appear.

To clear the question:

1. Click on the page in the Title Explorer and add an action. It will default to none.

2. Change the action to Reset Question.

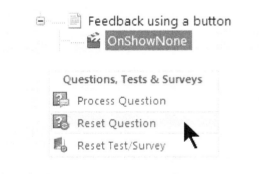

3. Change the condition for the action to run if the question Is Not Correct.

To Show Feedback Only If Incorrect and Enable the Next Button

4. Click on the Page in the Title Explorer and
    add these two actions.

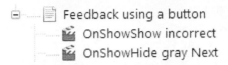

#	Name	Trigger	Action	Target	Condition
1	OnShowShow incorrect	Show	Show	incorrect text block	Question_0001 Is Not Correct
2	OnShowHide gray Next	Show	Hide	grayed-out Next btn	Question_0001 Is Not Empty

(Note that the above table is *not* a screen shot like most everything else is because I wanted to show the conditions. In Lectora the Condition column simply shows an icon if there is one, not the condition due to lack of room.)|

Speed Tip 8: Once you have one exercise working the way you want, try it out on some people to be sure it works for someone besides yourself. Then, instead of doing all this for your other exercises, just copy this page and paste it in where you want an exercise. Then change the text.

Assign Outside Activities

One final note which is really outside of Lectora is that you can always have the learner perform some outside activities such as trying something out or researching something and then have them return to the course and answer some questions.

Practice What You Learned

You learned a lot about making your course more engaging in this step. Before going on, take some time to create a few more pages and apply these techniques. Experiment with different options. This way what you have learned will stay with you.

Remember These Key Points

- Use Lectora's built-in activities to make the course more interesting. Remember the limitations:
  - Limited feedback
  - Not job related
  - No good way to show the correct answer when there are more than two choices
  - Most give the learner only two answer choices
  - **On Done Playing** action may not work
  - Spell check does not check the text
- Use Lectora's questions to help the learner apply the content in job settings.
- Give meaningful feedback.
- Don't frustrate the learner; make finding the correct answer a reasonable process.
- Restrict forward navigation *only* when absolutely necessary.
- Remember to add actions so that the page is meaningful when learners return to it.

To learn more about how to create effective exercises that are thought-provoking and how to make your course motivating, get a copy of *Designing Effective e-Learning: A Step-by-Step Guide* by Benjamin Pitman.

Remember, if you want the Lectora Title that I used to create this book with **working examples**, go to www.eProficiency.com/101.html.

Step 7: Add the Rest of Your Content

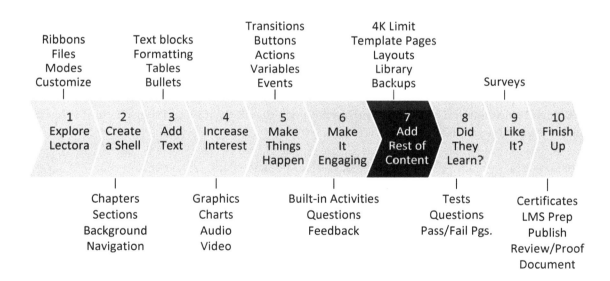

By now, you have learned how to add most of your content. You are probably already starting to put the rest of your content into the course. Before you do, there are a few things that you should attend to make your life easier.

Here's what you do in this step.

Make Sure Things Work	All browsers and computers are not equal. Before you get too far down the road, try your course out everywhere you plan for it to be used. Also, make sure it works within the limitations of the 4K limit and 508 requirements.
Use Good Design	While this is not a book on instructional design, there are still a few things you can do as you add material to make your course better.
Learn to Do Things Faster	You don't need to reinvent the wheel on every page. Apply these time-tested tips and tricks to meet your deadlines.
Back Up	Yes, back up your work. There are several ways to do this and I highly recommend them all. They have saved my assets more than once.

Make Sure Things Work

If you are doing this for yourself, then skip this step. But, if there are others involved, you need to check things out and adapt your course to the environment it will run in—your stakeholders, technical limitations, and your learners.

Try Out Your Prototype

If this is your first course, create a course with a few pages of content and a couple of simple exercises, a sample test and survey (if you have one) and get it to work properly before trying to do a 100 page 10mb course. Then run it by different people. Ask what would they change? What did they have problems with?

Stakeholders	Get your boss, course sponsor, client, customer to try it.
Techies	Then make sure your IT department can load it to the right place and you can get the desired reports regarding course completion, emails if any work, etc. There is no point in having a survey if you can't get the results.
Communications Dept.	They should have already signed off on your course, but if you have one, get them to sign off again making sure that it meets all their requirements for fonts, colors, branding, etc.

Target Learners	Get several target learners to try it from wherever it will be when in production (server, LMS, CD, etc.). Make sure you get a good cross section.
Target Browsers	Be sure to try it on all target browsers. If this is an internal course and learners will only use the company browser, you are good to go. But, if you are making this available to the public, be sure to try it with the most frequently used browsers and platforms: IE 6, 7, 8, 9, …, Google Chrome, FireFox, Mozilla, etc. Windows® XP, 7, 8, …, Mac, mobile devices like iPads, droids, etc.

While Lectora is a graphic layout tool (WYSIWYG), you should be aware that after publishing things may change and in fact may look different on different browsers.

 Warning 25: There are more than **40 differences** between what you see and how a page behaves in Lectora Edit, Run, Preview modes, Published as an Executable and what you see and how a page behaves when viewed through a browser. So, before you go copying a page over and over again, view the page through *all* potential browsers to be sure things still look right and works the same. Go to www.eProficiency.com/webStore/ and search for "differences" to get a list of more than 40 differences.

If you can't get it to work on your LMS, try it on the cloud on SCORM.com. It is free. That will tell you if the problem is in your course *or* in the LMS. If it works there but not on your LMS, let your IT staff know.

Doing this with a small course will keep you from having to make huge expensive time-consuming changes later and possibly disappoint some people.

Repeat this process any time you try something new like using large videos or Flash files.

Adapt to the 4K Hidden Limit

This applies to longer courses, ones over say 10 or 15 pages. You should plan on the learner getting interrupted, closing the course, and coming back later to finish it. By the way, research has shown that the e-learning courses that are the **most successful** in being completed and changing what people do **are the short ones. Long courses tend not to get finished or the information is not retained.**

So, if you have a course with a lot of questions in it, you need to be aware that there are limits to how much information can be retained between sessions (information like the answers to questions). Retained information includes things like answers to completed exercises or answered questions that are kept between sessions.

Publishing to Web (HTML)

If you do not have an LMS but plan to publish to Web (HTML) so your course is loaded on a network and run using a simple link, then you have several things to consider.

- If you are publishing to Web (HTML), you are limited to 4,096 characters of retained information like answers to questions. This information is stored in something called a "cookie" by the browser.

- If someone else uses the same computer and logs on as the same user of that computer, then that person will end up using the same cookie and it will look to them like they have already been in the course.

- There is no built-in bookmarking capability when you publish this way. You can build some yourself and it would be stored in the browser "cookie." Techniques to do that are covered in *Lectora 301: Techniques for Professionals* as well as being able to purchase them directly from www.eProficiency.com/webStore/ and search for "bookmark". So, be sure you let your learners know that if they exit the course before finishing, they will have to start from the beginning unless they make a note of where they left off and you give them a way to get at least close to that point using a Menu or Table of Contents.

Publishing to SCORM or AICC

When you publish to one of these, your Learning Management System will hold the retained information between sessions. AICC and SCORM 1.2 both have a 4K limit. The limit for SCORM 2004 is 64,000 characters. The LMS will do the bookmarking automatically if you select that option when you publish the course.

Publishing to an Executable File

If you plan to publish to a single executable file, you have the capability of bookmarking by right clicking on the course icon at the bottom of the screen and setting a bookmark. Retained variable information is stored in the Windows® registry (not a cookie) so you can store a lot more than the 4K you can in a cookie.

Reducing the Amount of Information Retained

There are several things you can do to reduce the amount of storage required to resume your course.

- Don't retain variables unless you really need to.
- Use short variable *names* but still make them meaningful.
  - Change question variable names from "Question_00xx" to "Qxx". (that saves 10 characters on each question)
- Use short variable *values*. Instead of "finished" and "not finished" use 0 and 1 or "y" and "n".

- This next tip can save you thousands of characters and allow you to have well over 100 questions instead of 30-40. In multiple-choice and multiple response questions:
  - Code the answer choices as just A, B, C, D in the Question Creator (wizard).
  - After finishing the wizard, click on each answer choice text block and check the Initially Hidden property so the student does not see them. Move them out of the way as no one will ever see them.
  - Then create a text block with the real answers and line the radio buttons or check boxes next to the correct answers.
  - This works fine unless you show the Results page at the end of your test. Then you really need to use the complete answers in the question wizard.
  - Ex. "Question_0001=Coaching the individual;" takes 38 characters; recoded to "Q01=a;" takes 7.
- Do not retain the information in short answer or essay questions.
- When you publish your course, choose the "short names" option. It may already be chosen for you.

 Warning 26: If your course does have more than 4K of retained information, it will behave unpredictably for your learners.

Does Your Course Need to Accessible by Individuals with Disabilities?

Does your course have to be 508 or WCAG 2.0 Compliant? If so, then:

1. On the Design ribbon, check the Use Web Accessibility Settings option in the Title Options.

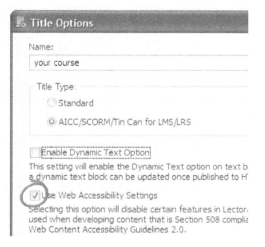

2. After you have a few pages developed, go to the Tools ribbon and click the Accessibility Check icon in the Review group. This tool will check your course for being compliant with the regulations.

If you need more information, click the Help button at the bottom of the compliance check window. You should do this frequently to avoid having to make many corrections.

Use Good Design

To the right is an overview of a typical course. It consists of one Assignable Unit (A001) that is created when you select AICC/SCORM ... in the Title Options on the Design ribbon.

The *hidden objects* are the navigation and background objects.

The Welcome/Splash page may contain some unusual graphics or a welcome video for example.

All the content is in one Chapter divided into topics using the Lectora Sections. It usually consists of some introduction pages followed by the course topics in Sections and concluded with a wrap-up Section.

The Popups Chapter contains any popup pages you may have.

The Development Only Chapter holds template pages and objects that are used to develop and update the course.

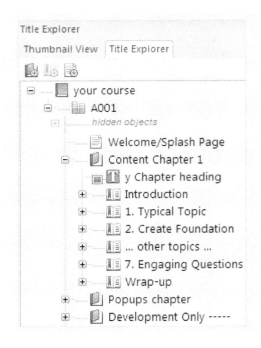

Try These Recommended Introduction Pages

Here are some useful pages to put in the Introduction. More details can be found in the book, *Designing Effective e-Learning: A Step-by-Step Guide* by Benjamin Pitman.

- Introduction
  - Welcome
  - How to Navigate
  - Introduction
  - Why Take This Training
  - Expectations
  - Course Overview
  - About the Pretest
  - Opening Questions
  - Main Menu

Welcome page	Here is one place where it is worth spending some hours on good graphics. It usually has the course name, revision number, date, and copyright.
How to Navigate page	You might also provide information about optimal viewing of the course like setting the browser zoom factor to 100%, popup blockers, etc.
Course Introduction page	This page might include a very brief description of the course, whom it was designed for, its purpose/goal, prerequisites, estimated time to complete, if there is a test, etc.
Why Take This Training (Benefits) page	Answer the question, "Why should I take this course?" or "What's in it for me?" List as many personal benefits as possible.
Expectations (Objectives) page	Spell out what is expected of the learner after completing this course. This will increase motivation and learning.
Pretest Info page	Some courses have a pretest. If you do, spell out what it is for.
Course Overview page	This page and its cousins the topic overview pages are some of the most important yet frequently omitted pages. These pages help learners see your approach and begin to organize the material in their mind.
Opening Questions page	This page can pose some thought provoking questions to help the learner focus on the content.
Main Menu page	Some longer courses can make good use of a main menu page.

Use the Right Pages in Your Topics

A typical topic should begin with an overview of the topic explaining how the content is organized and how it fits in to the whole course.

You may have some specific detailed objectives for this module specifying what is expected of learners when they finish this topic.

This is followed by several content pages. To help learners master the material, you should have an exercise every 3-7 pages of content where you *apply* what was just covered to real-world situations, not just have them recall it.

At the end of the topic is a summary of the major points. Remember that summaries should not just list the topics but resemble a job aid.

What's in the Wrap-up Chapter?

If you had opening questions to peak learners, return to them and provide answers. You could even ask for their ideas and then give them the official version of the answers.

Once all the material has been covered, wrap-up with an overall course summary highlighting the most important points.

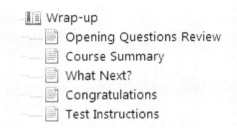

If you do have a test

You might have a page introducing the test and explaining how the grading works.

If you don't have a test

You might have a page telling the student what to do next – check with boss, take next course in the series, etc.

You might have a congratulations page.

- On the *last* page of the course, somehow disable the Next button. A common way to do that is to Exclude it from being inherited.

  On the Properties ribbon for the page, click Inherit.

In the Inheritance Settings dialog window,

- select Specific objects from parents
- then click on any navigation object that would take the learner to the next page and move them to the Excluded side by clicking on the >>>.

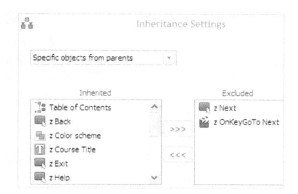

Organize Your Popup Pages

The Popups Chapter holds all the popup pages you might have in your course. I recommend that you put popup pages for a specific topic in their own Section as shown here. It makes a lot easier to find them when needed.

You may have a Section for glossary terms.

And you may have some global popups. Here are a few ideas.

- The About page should have the date the course was published along with other course relevant info.

- The Contact Us page is useful to give students a way to ask questions as well as let you know about issues with the course.

- The Contents page is a table of contents allowing the learners to roam around the course at will.

- The Documents page lists any reference documents you want the learners to have access to in one place.

- The Exit page confirms whether or not they want to exit from the course. While some people use it, I do *not* recommend it as it is a bit tricky to set up the proper actions when using an LMS.

The Printable Course Summary is just that. It can be a Lectora page or better yet, a PDF in which case I would put it on the Documents page.

Learn to Do Things Faster

In this section, we will cover some of the more common things you can do to speed up your development. You will find even more in my book, Lectora 201.

Make Mass Changes with Find and Replace

On the Home ribbon you will see Find and Replace in the Edit group. Here you can make mass changes to text like you can in other applications. See *Lectora 201: What They Don't Tell You in Class* for ways to do faster if you have large courses and need to make lots of changes.

Select Multiple Objects

There are a couple of ways to select multiple objects for changing all their properties at once, copying, saving to the Library, or aligning. You can:

- In the Title Explorer, hold the Ctrl key down and click on them individually. They must all be at the same level (on the same page, at the Section level, the Chapter level, or Title level).

- In the Title Explorer, click on one item, hold the Shift key down, and click on another item. This selects *all* the objects from the first to the last. Again, they must all be at the same level.

- In the layout pane, hold the Ctrl key down and click on objects individually. They must all be at the same level.

- In the layout pane, click just outside one object and drag until all desired objects are selected. *Note that they do not all have to be at the same level with this technique which makes it very handy for aligning objects at different levels.*

Change Properties of Multiple Objects At One Time

Speed Tip 9: One of the nice new things with Lectora 11 is that you can select a number of objects and change the *common properties* of all of them at the same time.

- For text objects, you can change all the font characteristics at one time.

- For several Lectora shapes, you can change the color, border, etc. at one time.

- For a mixed set of shapes, you can only change the properties that they have in common.

Copy and Paste Three Ways

You have three ways you can copy and paste, two of which do *not* involve the clipboard.

1. Traditional Cut/Copy and Paste
    (all these techniques use the clipboard)

    Click on the desired object either in the Title Explorer or the layout pane. Then cut/copy and paste by using either:

    – Right click menu (takes a while to move your cursor to the right choice)

    – Click on the icons in the upper left of the Lectora window

    – Modify the Quick Access Toolbar and put the icons on it (not much gained)

    – Use keyboard shortcuts of Ctrl+X (cut), Ctrl-C (copy), and Ctrl-V (paste)

    – Use Ctrl+Shift+V to paste *unformatted* text.

Paste Unformatted

2. Click and drag

    This does *not* use the clipboard so you can have one object copied to the clipboard while copying another.

    Click on the object in the Title Explorer.

    – If you drag it, to another page, it will effectively cut it from the original page and paste it into the new page.

    – If you hold the Ctrl key down while dragging, a small + sign in a box will appear (Windows® standard) indicating you are making a copy, not moving the original.

3. Use the Media Library

   Right click and select **Save as Library Object**.
   Then you can just drag it out of the **My Library**
   any time you need it without using the
   clipboard.

Use Mouse Shortcuts

Speed Tip 10: You can:

- Double click on any object in the **Title Explorer** and quickly show the **Properties**
  ribbon.

- Double click on any object in the layout pane except a text block and show its
  Properties ribbon.

Speed Tip 11: You can *right* click on most any object and get a long list of options rather than hunt for the right ribbon.

Keep the Title Explorer Organized

- Arrange of objects in the **Title Explorer** in a logi-
  cal order from the top of the screen to the bottom because:

  - It speeds up development because it makes
    it easier to find things.

  - Screen readers read the text in that order.

  - When you export the course for translation,
    the text appears in this order.

  - When you export the course to MS Word®,
    the text appears in this order.

- From time to time, right-click in the **Title Ex-**
  plorer on the topmost line and select **Collapse
  All**. Then expand back to the area you were
  working on. This will keep you from getting
  lost.

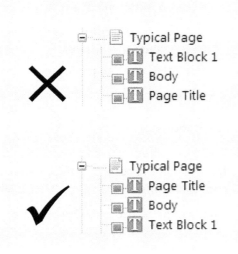

Use Effective Naming Conventions

Here are some naming conventions that will make your course easier to understand and faster to
code.

Identify Which Level the Object Belongs To

Put a "z" as the first character of all Title level actions and objects. That way when you go to Exclude them from being inherited, they are all grouped *together separate* from other inherited objects. More importantly, when you go to select Targets when creating actions it makes all these objects appear at the *together at the bottom* of the list making the more commonly referenced objects on the page easier to find at the top of the list. Example: "z Next" for the Next button.

Put a "y" prefix on Chapter level items and an "x" on Section level items. Again, this keeps all the Chapter items together and all the Section level items together in the Inheritance panel and when selecting the Target for actions.

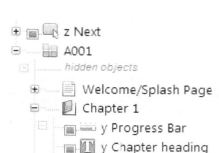

Clarify the Contents of Groups

Begin the group name with either "actions- " or "objects- ". Follow that with a capital letter of the rest of the name. Examples: "actions- Common feedback" and "objects- Feedback". Then in the Title Explorer, put all the action groups together in alphabetic order and all the object groups as close together as possible based on layering with other objects. This makes it sooooo much easier to find stuff when coding Actions or making changes.

Other Naming Conventions:

Suppose you have three buttons on the screen that are to be clicked or moused over by the learner to show more information. Each button Shows and Hides different text blocks and pictures. Code everything with similar names but differentiate by prefixing or appending a 1, 2, or 3 to each object. That way I can create the actions for the first set and then copy and paste them to the other buttons and just change the targets which will be readily locatable when opening the Target property.

Here is a snipit of the dropdown list when creating a Show action. Notice how all the objects are grouped together and the Title level ones are at the bottom, then the Chapter ones, then the Section ones. This way the ones you want most frequently are closest to the top.

1 audio
1 Play
1 Stop
1 Pause
2 audio
2 Play
2 bullet
3 bullet

1 audio
1 Pause
1 Play
1 Stop
2 audio
2 bullet
2 Pause
2 Play
3 bullet

x Section heading
y Chapter heading

z Back
z Course Title
z Exit

Use the Lectora Library

If you do much Lectora development work, using the My Library can save you tons of time and improve the consistency of the look and feel of your courses. Most developers either don't know about it or use it in way below capacity. Fortunately, Lectora 11 has made it even easier to use.

You can save most any object or set of objects you use in Lectora as a Library Object for reuse in future courses.

- A graphic image

- A single text block

- Several text blocks and images

- A group of objects

- An action or several actions

- A page or several pages

- A Section, Chapter, Title

- Lots more

You can *not* create a Library Object from a *part* of a question.

Prepare Your Object

While this is not absolutely necessary, these tips will make your Library Objects more usable.

 Warning 27: Variable Names: While you can save questions and form objects, know that when they are reused later they will create a new variable name *if the one in the Library Object is already in use*. Examples:

- You save a drop-down list box and the variable name is DropList_0001. Later you use it again in the same Title. Lectora will assign it a new variable name, DropList_0002 if you have no other drop-down list boxes.

- You save a multiple-choice question with the variable name of QA. Later you use that same question twice in a new Title. The first time it will use the variable name of QA. The second time you use it, Lectora will change the variable name to Question_0xxx, where xxx is the next available question number.

Addressing this issue is part of preparing your object.

Prepare your object by:

- Clearly labeling each object and action as to what it does. When you use the object later, you may have forgotten some of how it works. For more complicated actions and other things, be sure to make use of the object description by clicking on the downward diagonal arrow in the first group of the ribbon for that object.

- Using unique names for variables where Lectora generates the variable name – questions and form objects. This is how you get around the Lectora renaming variables issue. Lectora will *not* rename a variable if it is *not* already in use. i.e. it will use your variable name the *first* time. Then what you do is open the question or form object properties and change it to something unique in that Title. Lectora will change all references to your variable name. Then you can bring in another copy of that Library Object.

Use variable names like _Qx or _LibQx

- Flagging objects that need to be changed (like the ones that have special variable names or maybe need a condition changed) with special names. Making an arrow is one good way to make the object stand out and remind you that it needs to be changed.

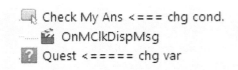

Create Your Library Object

1. Select the objects you want to be part of single Library Object.

2. Right click and select **Save as Library Object**.

3. Enter the desired name in the dialog window that opens.

Warning 28: Do not use any of the prohibited characters for a Windows® file name (/*?:<>|.) when you name your Library object. You get a strange error message like this if you do.

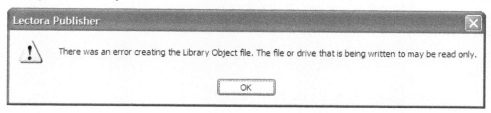

Your object is now readily available by clicking My Library and then opening the Library Objects folder.

Insert a Library Object

1. Click on an object or page *after which* you want the Library Object to go. This controls the layering. The inserted object will be in front of the select object.

2. Then click on the My Library tab on the right side of the layout pane. It will open and you can just double click on the Library Object you want and it will be inserted *after* the item you clicked on in #1 above.

Import Pages from PowerPoint® or Other Titles

There are a couple of other ways you can create pages other than building them from scratch or using templates, Library objects, or example pages. You can:

- Import pages from a PowerPoint® presentation.

- Import pages from another Title.

Importing Pages from PowerPoint®

You can import pages from PowerPoint® using the From PowerPoint® tool on the Tools ribbon.

Once you open the file, another dialog window allows you to specify which pages you want to import.

If you change the size of the pages you are importing from 1024x768, then Lectora will scale objects, spacing, and fonts up or down as needed. This does not always give desirable results. You may have to go through every page and make adjustments.

The imported pages go in to a new Chapter at the end of your Title. Now just copy the pages and paste them to where you want them in your new Title.

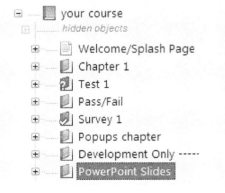

There is a good use for this tool but you have to do a little prework and a couple more steps. You can use PowerPoint® as your storyboard tool and then import the contents directly into Lectora.

1. Before you build anything in PowerPoint®, create your Lectora Title shell with one blank page. Include all the navigation and background images.

2. Take a screen snapshot of a blank page and use it as the background in PowerPoint® on a Master page.

3. Then build your storyboard using fonts and text blocks the same as you would in Lectora.
   - If you use the PowerPoint® title block, it will come in as the Lectora Page title in the Title Explorer as well as text blocks on the page.
   - Arrange things how you want them to be in Lectora.
   - Put all your notes in the Notes section in PowerPoint®, not as text blocks on the page. These will come in as Notes in Lectora.

4. After all your storyboard reviews, import the storyboard into Lectora.

Importing Pages from Another Title

You can use the From Other Title tool in the Import group of the Tools ribbon. When you click it, a dialog window opens and you can navigate to another Title.

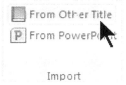

Once you select another Title, another dialog window allows you to specify which Chapters, Sections, Pages, or objects you want to import. The new objects will appear at the end of your current Title.

Note that you can do the same thing by opening the other Title, copying what you want ,and then pasting it into your new presentation.

Add More Pages

Now you are finally ready to add more pages. You can:

- Simply add more blank pages and format them as you go, or
- Use Page Layouts to save a little time, or
- Use the Lectora Library, or
- Copy and paste pages.

Adding Blank Pages

If all you want to do is add blank pages, then follow these instructions.

You can add blank pages by clicking on the Page icon.

- You can click on the down arrow of Page icon in the Home ribbon. You get a dropdown list with a wide choice of page layouts. You can select one. (We will cover these later when we talk about creating professional looking pages.)

- Or you can click on the upper portion of the icon, you get the last layout you selected.

- Or you can click Page icon in the Title Explorer which works the same way.

Lectora will add a new page to your course immediately after whatever is currently selected in the Title Explorer.

Using Lectora Page Layouts

What is a Page Layout? Page Layouts contain placeholders for the most common Lectora objects like text blocks, images, audio, video, and animation. The text blocks can be preformatted to use specific font and numbering or bullets. They do *not* contain paragraph spacing or line spacing.

1. To create, change, or use a page layout, click on the down arrow on bottom part of the Page icon on the Home ribbon.

2. Click on any one of the built in page layouts in the dropdown list to use that layout. Try several different ones to see what they are like.

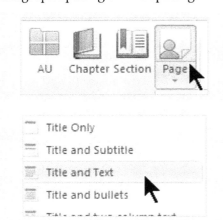

3. Click on Manage Page Layout at the bottom to import, export, or delete a layout.

4. You can create a new layout by simply saving the current page.

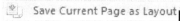

Speed Tip 12: Start with a layout you like for your most common page. Tweak it till you have it the way you want it. Then select Save Current Page as Layout from the Page dropdown list. If you start your layout name with an underscore (_), then it will appear at the top of the list. Now you can easily apply that layout to all your new pages.

You can save your layouts by exporting them one at a time. Click on the Page dropdown list and select Manage Page Layout … Then in the dialog window, click on the layout you want to export and click the Export button.

Warning 29: That is the good news. Unfortunately, page layouts have several limitations.

- They do not seem to carry over *text block* properties like borders, margins, background color, transitions, etc.
- They do not currently carry over paragraph or line spacing.
- They do not seem to retain any *page* properties such as background color. They do inherit everything as you would expect.
- They do not seem to carry over any actions attached to a text block or the page.
- You can only export *one* at a time for backup.
- And finally, pages created with a layout will *not* change when the layout is changed. You have to manually go to each page and change it.

Using the Lectora Library

Well, you can see that Page Layouts are nice but leave a lot to be desired. So, how do you make the rest of your pages have the same look as the one you just spent so much time on without repeating all that work? You can either use a Library Object or simply copy and paste an existing page.

A page saved to the Library and reused solves most of the problems just mentioned.

You start by saving the page you just laid out.

1. Just right click in a blank area of the page and select Save as Library Object.

Then when you want to insert that page:

2. First click on the page *after* which you want the page inserted. If you click on a Chapter or a Section, it will become the first page in that Chapter or Section.

3. Click the My Library tab on the right of the screen.

4. Double click on the page you want to insert.

Library Objects do have a few limitations. If there is any connection on the page to the current Title such as links, action groups, or excluded objects (see Working with Inheritance on page 42), then these will not be carried over.

Copying a Page

Probably the best way is to simply copy and paste a page and then modify it. However, this usually means that you have to delete all the objects that are on there now. Instead, do this.

1. Add a Chapter at the end of your course and call it something like Development Only. Use this Chapter to hold pages never shown to learners but are just used for development.

2. Then create page templates with whatever objects you want on that page. When you need a page with those characteristics, just copy it from the Development Only Chapter and paste to where you need it. These pages will keep all references to higher level objects including actions that reference Title and Chapter level objects.

You can also have pages with commonly used graphics. You can put them in the Lectora Library which I do frequently but sometimes they work better if I leave them in the course as they have links to some part of the course.

Back Up Your Work

Backups with Lectora are a little different from with other applications. While you can back up most of your work, there are a few things that are not backed up unless you do something special. These include your text styles, page layouts, library objects, and published strings.

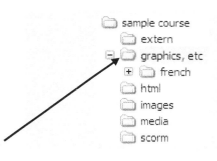

Back Up Your Course Folder

You should back up your course every hour. In fact, you should back up *any* document you work on regardless of the application every hour to prevent accidental loss.

Just as a reminder, I recommend that you keep all your course related documents and graphics in the same main folder or subfolders within your course folder so they get backed up too. Here they are in the "graphics, etc" folder.

- If you have WinZip or something like it, you can set it up to run every hour and back up certain folders. You can have it append the date and time to the backup so you can go back as far as needed.

- You may be able to set something up using .BAT files and the Windows® Scheduler Tasks if you know how. Check with your IT department and tell them you want to archive specific folders every hour. Maybe they can help.

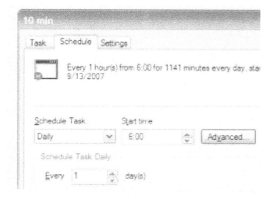

- Going beyond simply saving to your hard drive, you need to back up your files to an external source. If you work in a company that backs up its servers regularly, then move a copy of your course to the server daily. One good way is to zip the entire course folder and then add today's date to the name. Use that for your backup. That way you can create a history of your course. Later on when your course is in production, you can delete the early backups.

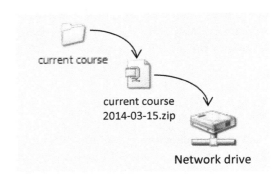

- If you don't have that option, backup to an external hard drive yourself. Better yet, use one of the online cloud backup services now available like Dropbox or SugarSync. This way you are covered even if your work location goes up in smoke and destroys not only your computer but also your backup drives.

Export Your Text Styles

Text Styles are global and are *not* included in your ccurse folder. You have to take extra steps to back them up. You only need to do this when your Text Styles change.

1. Click on a text block and then click on Text Style on the Home ribbon.

2. Select Manage Styles from the dropdown list.

3. Click on the top style, hold the **Shift** key down and click on the bottom style to select them all.

4. Click **Export Styles** and save them to somewhere that will be backed up. You might want to put them in same folder with your course.

Export Page Layouts

If you have page layouts you use a lot, you should back them up too. Unfortunately, as of April, 2013, there is no easy way to export them all. You click on the **Page** icon on the **Home** ribbon, click on **Manage Page Layouts**, and then, one at a time, select a layout and export it. This is another reason for saving the common layouts in a Development Only **Chapter** in the course.

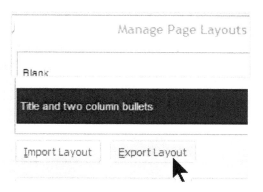

Back Up Your Library Objects

Currently there is no easy way to put **Library Objects** in any location other than somewhere in the Program Files folder. If you have a hard disk failure or get a virus and need to rebuild your drive these may be lost because they are not normally backed up (not part of your My Documents folder). So, if you put objects into the Library you want backed up, you have to copy them to where they will be.

1. First create a folder where you want to keep a copy of the library objects where it will be backed up.

2. Right click on any object in My Library and select Show in Windows Explorer.

3. Copy all the objects in the Lectora Library by
   selecting them all (Ctrl+A) and then either right
   click and Copy or Ctrl+C.

4. Switch to the new folder you created and paste
   (Ctrl+V) or right click and paste.

Backup Your Publish Strings

You can change the automatic messages that are displayed from time to time by Lectora when
your course is running. Some people like to make these more learner-friendly. If you change any
of these, Be sure to Export them using File menu > Preferences > Publish Strings and then back them
up. Like Text Styles, you only need to do this when they change.

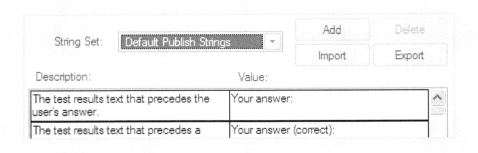

Practice What You Learned

You learned a lot about adding the rest of your content in this
step. Before going on, take some time to apply these techniques
before you go on. Experiment with different options. This way
what you have learned will stay with you.

Remember These Key Points

- Use My Library or simply copy template Pages from your Development Chapter to add more Pages to your course.

- An easy-to-use structure for your course is this. ➜

- Use pages in the introduction that tell the student what the course is about, why it is important to them, how it relates to other courses in the series, how it is organized, what is expected of them after completion, and give them some things to be thinking about before they start.

- In each topic:
  - begin with an overview,
  - have exercises every 3-7 pages that apply the content to their jobs, and
  - end each topic with a summary.

- Wrap-up the course with an overall summary and explain what is next.

- If you have a test, have a test outcome Chapter with passed and failed pages showing test score along with what they need to do next.

Step 8: See If They Learned Anything with Tests

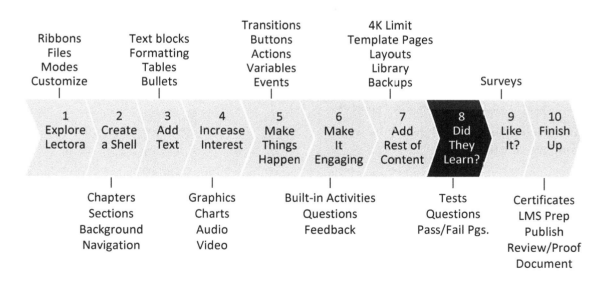

Sometimes you will have a test in your course. When you do encounter that, be prepared to do a bit more work than just add a few questions in a Chapter.

In this step, you have several things you need to do to use a Test properly. You:

Add a Test Chapter	Add a special type of Chapter to hold your test and grade it.
Add a Pass/Fail Chapter	Add a Chapter with pages to land on after the test is over and that tell the learners what to do next.
Configure a Test	Specify Test behavior and what results are to be presented, add questions, handle randomization and grading.
Create a Pass/Fail Chapter	Once the test is over, you will need somewhere for the learners to land to get their instructions on what to do next.

Add a Test Chapter

1. Begin by clicking on your content Chapter in the Title Explorer. This will ensure that the test is placed after your content.

2. Click on the Text & Survey ribbon and then click on the Test icon in the Add Test or Survey group.

Lectora will add a Test after your content.

We will need one more thing before we can configure the test.

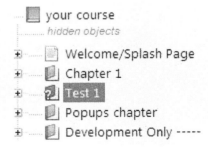

Create a Pass/Fail Chapter

When we configure the Test next, we will need to specify where to go when learners pass the test or fail the test

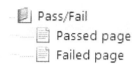

1. Add a Chapter after the Test.

2. Make it have two pages, one for when learners pass the test and one for when they fail. These pages tell learners whether they passed or not and give them instructions about what to do next.

3. Be sure to disable the navigation to the next page on both of these pages.

4. You also may want to change the Back button action from Previous Page to Back because if they land on the Failed page, Previous Page will take them to the Passed page whereas Back will take them to the last page in the test.

Consider including the following items on these pages.

Item	Example
Greeting words with the learner's name	Passed: "Congratulations Mary!" Failed: "Sorry Mary, you did not pass this Knowledge Check." ("You did not pass" is better than "You failed.")
Test score	The final score shown as a %, a letter grade, a number of points earned out of a possible maximum, the number of questions right out of the total asked or some combination of these
Passing score	"You needed a score of 80% to pass."
Section scores	If you had Test Sections, it may be helpful to learners to know which sections (objectives or topics) they need to study more. You could display the score for each Section on these pages.
Text that ties score back to expectations (objectives) or course goal	Passed: "It looks like you have learned enough to effectively coach a chronically late employee." Failed: "It looks like you might have trouble effectively coaching a chronically late employee."

Item	Example
Instructions as to what to do next	Passed: "Click Next to proceed to the next coaching topic." Failed: "Please click the button below to review this information again and retake this test."

Configure the Test

Tests include their own navigation buttons and *exclude* everything from the Title – i.e. they do not inherit any objects like navigation, titles, etc.

 Best Practice 21: It is good practice to use the same navigation and page numbering as you used in your Content Chapter so learners do not have to be figuring out how to navigate at the same time they are taking a stressful test.

You may want to do something a *little* different like change the heading or use an icon like a large question mark that is inherited on all the pages.

Making It Look Like the Rest of the Course

We begin by doing a few things that will make it look like it belongs to the course.

1. Expand the Test Chapter and delete the page count and the navigation objects shown.

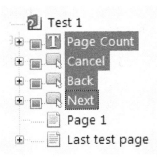

2. A standard test defaults to inheriting no objects from parents, which means you have nothing at this point including navigation as we just deleted the defaults. You need to change that by going to the Test Properties ribbon and changing what is inherited.

3. Click on Inherit and open the inheritance window. There change the dropdown box from NO objects to ALL objects.

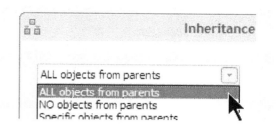

Making the Test Different

While the test pages should look like the rest of the course for the most part, you may want to do something different to let them know they are in a test.

You could add a question mark or some other icon to indicate that this is a test. Or maybe you have change the page heading. Put these at the Test level and they will be inherited by all the pages.

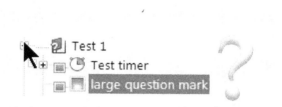

Specifying the Test Behavior

Tests really have *three* Properties ribbons, one for the usual Properties, one for how the Test behaves, and one for what and how results are shown.

The properties on the Behavior ribbon specify how the test will react while the student is taking the test.

These include:

- Whether or not feedback is shown

- Whether the student must answer the question before proceeding

- Whether to retain answers between sessions

- What to do when the test is over

- Whether or not to select the questions randomly

- Timing the test

It is a good idea to go over these and the Results options with your course sponsor.

To specify Test Behavior:

1. Begin by clicking on the Behavior tab to set the desired options.

2. In the first area, check the Show Feedback .for Each Question if you want the question feedback to show. This is a global property and even if you have *checked* Enable Feedback on the individual questions, the feedback will *not* be shown.

   If you want to force students to answer the questions before proceeding, check that property.

   If you want to allow the student to exit the course and return and see their answers, check the Retain Answers Between Sessions. See Adapt to the 4K Hidden Limit on page 179 before you do this for large tests.

3. In the On Completed/Passed group, change the Target to be the Passed page.

   In the On Cancelled/Failed group, change the Target to be the Failed page.

4. If you want Lectora to select your questions at random (to reduce cheating) you can check the Randomly Select Pages box and then select how many you want selected. See on Randomizing Questions and Answers on page 217 for more on this topic.

Timed Tests

1. If you want a timed test, check the last box. When the timer expires, the test will be processed which includes:
   - displaying the results you specified on the Test Results ribbon and
   - performing the passed or failed actions.

2. If you elected a timed test, you need to set how much time students have. Click on the newly added Test timer and drag it to the desired location on the page.

3. Then on its Properties ribbon, you can specify the amount of time in hours, minutes, and seconds as well as what will be shown in the timer.

4. In the Style group, you can specify the text properties of the timer.

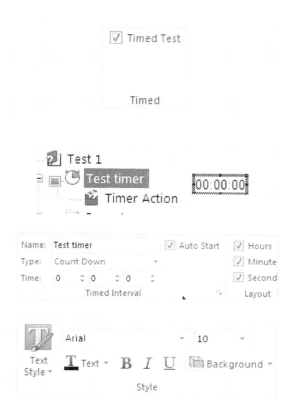

Specifying Test Results

When your test is processed, it is scored and you can have the results displayed. You can also submit the results to somewhere other than the LMS. You set these options on the Test Results ribbon.

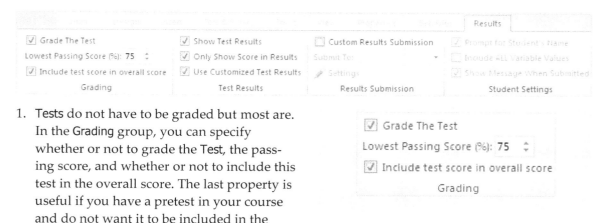

1. **Tests** do not have to be graded but most are. In the Grading group, you can specify whether or not to grade the Test, the passing score, and whether or not to include this test in the overall score. The last property is useful if you have a pretest in your course and do not want it to be included in the overall score.

Three Ways to Set a Passing Score

Horton (2006) suggests three ways to set the passing score, which are summarized here. Start by considering the real-world consequences (dangers) of getting a less-than-perfect score. The less significant the consequences, the lower the passing score can be and the less rigorous you can be.

Professional judgment	(Okay)	Simply use professional judgment to set the score. This is really just a good guess and may be *hard to defend if challenged.*
Consensus of Experts	(Better)	Base the passing score on the consensus of several (three or more) experts in the field. Have them take the assessment before they give what they think should be a passing grade.
Contrasting groups	(Best)	Have a group of experienced people (at least 12) and a group of inexperienced people (at least 12) take the assessment. Determine the mean and standard deviation of the scores for each group. Set the passing score between one standard deviation below the experienced score and one standard deviation above the inexperienced group score. *If someone's pay depends on this test, this method is probably the best.*

2. In the Test Results group can you begin to specify what you want the students to see when they complete the Test. This is optional and you do not need to show this, especially if all you want to do is show the score and tell the student what to do next in the Pass/Fail Chapter. In that case, all you need is the Pass/Fail Chapter covered on page 218.

Checking Show Test Results will display a standard popup window with the score the question number and text, the learner's choice, and the correct answer.

☑ Show Test Results
☐ Only Show Score in Results
☐ Use Customized Test Results
Test Results

Test 1

Test 1

SCORE: 33%
FAILED

Question 1
Question Text
Your answer: False
Correct answer: True

Question 2

Checking Only Show Score in Results will only the score and nothing else.

☑ Show Test Results
☑ Only Show Score in Results
☐ Use Customized Test Results
Test Results

Test 1

Test 1

SCORE: 0%
FAILED

Checking **Use Customized Test Results** will show the test results in a **Page** you have more control over shows.

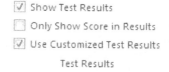

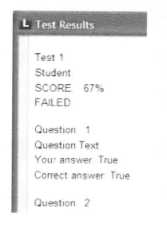

When you check the **Use Customized Test Results**, Lectora adds a new *red* page at the end of the **Test**.

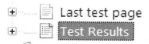

Now you can customize this **Page** to a limited extent by specifying what it shows using its **Content** ribbon that appears when you click on the page. Decide which of these you want by discussing with your team and the project sponsor. You can also format the text blocks to some degree including color, size, etc. as well as the layout of the page to some degree. If you use randomization, be sure to double check how this looks in HTML as well as previewed in the course.

3. By default, your test score is submitted to your LMS if you are using one. If you have elected to **Retain Answers** between sessions on the **Behavior** ribbon, then the answer to *each* question is also sent to your LMS. You may need your IT staff to create queries to retrieve these data. By checking the **Custom Results Submission**, you can also have these results sent to other places.

The results are sent to the same server from which the course was launched and then processed by a specified script on that server, sent to an email address, or a Google Drive. Usually these are written by your IT staff. You can find one for PHP email for a Linux or UNIX server on www.eProficiency.com/webStore/ and search for "linux". If you want to post the results to a database other than your LMS, consult your IT staff.

Adding Questions

We have covered how to add questions and the different types back in Step 6: Make Your Course Engaging on page 153. You add questions to a Test in the same way, however, in a Test, there are a few things to consider:

- Question phrasing
- Question weight
- Types of questions that are gradable
- Feedback
- Returning to the page

Question Phrasing

Yes, this is a test and its goal is to see if learners can recall what they learned. However, don't give in to the temptation to make the questions be *simple recall* questions. Make the questions *applied* so the learners have more practice applying the information to the real world. Remember to make them second-person questions using "you".

Example: "A team member starts to dominate a meeting. What would you do?"

Question Weight

Avoid partial credit on any given question because explaining how the score is computed can get hairy. Consider a multiple-choice response question or a drag and drop one. Why don't they take off for wrong answers? I can barely understand how all this works. It is better to just weigh each question one point. If you do otherwise, you are obligated to explain the scoring mechanism to the student and that can cause some real frustration. Your goal is for them to learn the content, not spend lots of energy understanding out how the test works. Leave the Point Value at 1 and Keep It Simple for the Student!

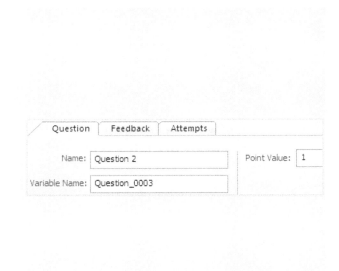

Gradable Questions

It is very easy to see which ones are gradable in the new Lectora when you select your question type.

Feedback

While some like to wait till the end of the test to give feedback, students learn more if they get feedback as they answer each question. It bonds the feedback to the question situation. If you wait till the end, all they are interested in is their score. Refer to Step 6: Step 6: Make Your Course Engaging for ideas on giving feedback.

Students Returning to the Page

When you created exercises, you were concerned about them returning and misinterpreting an incorrect answer for a correct one. That is not so true in a test. If you allow students to change their answers by coming back and reviewing the test, then you do *not* need to do this.

If however, you do want to *prevent students from changing their answer*, then use the Attempts tab in the Question Creator.

1. Click on the question in the Title Explorer.

2. Click on the Edit Attempts icon in the Question Properties ribbon.

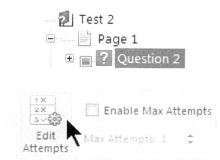

3. Check **Set Maximum Allowed Attempts** and **On Process Question** and leave **Enable Feedback** ... unchecked as shown here. As it says on this panel, "Setting maximum attempts will lock the question after the maximum number of attempts has been reached."

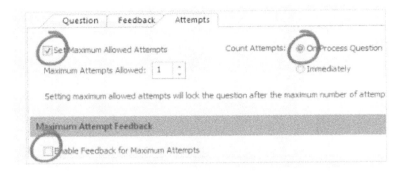

Now, the question will be locked when students either go to the next page or they click on a button that has a **Process Question** action on it.

Organizing Your Test Using Test Sections

If you have multiple topics in your course, you may want to divide your **Test** into **Sections** to be sure that you have sufficient questions for each topic or objective in the course.

1. Click on the **Test Chapter** and then add a **Section**. You *cannot* use the **Section** icon you normally would use at the top of the **Title Explorer**. You must click on the **Test & Survey** ribbon and then click the **Section** icon. Then add your questions to that **Section**. If you already have your questions and want to arrange them in **Sections**, you can just drag and drop them into the appropriate **Section**.

2. If you want, you can add an icon or heading in each **Section** that would identify which topic or objective the questions related to.

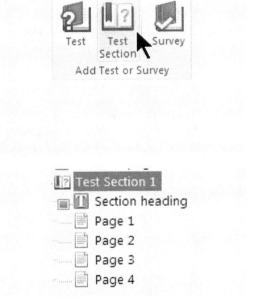

Once a test is processed, if you checked the **Grade The Test** property on the **Results** ribbon, each test **Section** will have its own grade.

Randomizing Questions and Answers

One way to reduce cheating is to use randomization. Lectora provides two types of randomization:

- One type randomizes the sequence in which *answer choices* appear in a specific question each time it is viewed.

- The other type selects a specific number of *questions* from a pool of questions and presents them to the learner in random order.

Randomizing Answer Choices

Some questions, like Multiple Choice and Multiple Response, have the option to randomize the sequence in which answer choices appear on the screen each time the question is viewed.

Question Text	Question Text	Question Text
○ Choice One	○ Choice Three	○ Choice Three
○ Choice Three	○ Choice Two	○ Choice One
○ Choice Two	○ Choice One	○ Choice Two

— Choices —

☑ Randomize choices ⓘ

To make this happen, check the Randomize choices property on the Question tab of the Question Creator. If it is grayed-out or does not appear, then it is choice randomization is not available for that question.

Make sure that all text blocks are big enough to hold *any* answer.

Randomizing Question Selection and Sequence

You can randomize the *entire* Test by clicking on the Randomly Select Pages from the Randomize group on the Behavior ribbon. For example, you may have a pool of 30 questions and want 10 selected at random.

☑ Randomly Select Pages

Pages From Test: 10 ↕

Randomize

You can randomize questions at the Test level, which selects questions from the entire Test.

- If you have **20** questions and randomly select 10 then Lectora will pick 10 questions at random and present them in random order.

- If you have **10** questions and select 10, then it will present *all* the questions in random order.

However, you may want to be more precise and select some questions from each of several pools. If you put them all in one Test, you are likely to get many questions for some objectives and few or none for others.

For example, suppose you have five objectives. You have created four questions for each objective and want at least two questions for each objective to show on the test to be sure that each objective is adequately covered on the test. You want them randomly selected from the four for that objective. Here's what you would do.

1. Create five test Sections with four questions in each.

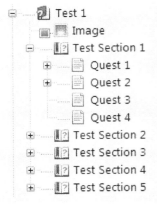

2. Click on each Section in the Title Explorer and then on the Behavior ribbon. Check the Randomly Select Pages and specify how many in the dropdown list. In each Section, you can have a different number of questions and specify a different number to be selected.

Now, when your test is presented to learners, they will see two questions selected at random from each Section.

Submitting the Test for Grading

What you need to do here depends a lot on if and how you have randomized the question sequence.

• If you randomized the entire Test,	then the test is *automatically graded* once the learner leaves the test.
• If you divided your Test into Sections and the last Section is randomized and *there are no other pages* after that,	then the test is *automatically graded* once the learner leaves the test.
• If the *entire* Test is *not* randomized and the last page of the Test is *not* in a randomized Section,	then you need an action on that last page to Process Test/Survey.

Frequently I have randomized Test Sections and then have one page after all of the questions where I have a "Submit Test for Grading" button and some instructions telling the student to either click the Submit button or click Back to review the test. At times I have even had a button to take them back to the beginning of the Test.

Configuring Questions, Sections, and Tests to Get the Right Average

You can use one or more Tests to see if they learned anything. Before we start into this complex topic, I recommend that you have just *one* Test in a course and when you see the need for a second Test, make it and its content a separate course.

Grading Rules

- Unanswered questions are treated as incorrect.

- The points from each question presented are added together

- The Test and Section scores = total points of correct answers divided by total points of questions selected expressed as a percentage.

- The Test score is based on all the questions in the Test, *not* an average of the Sections.

- Tests that have unchecked the Include test score in overall score are not included in the average test score.

There is a little bit more to know if you have more than one test in a course. See What You Need to Do If You Have a Test on page 234.

For example, if you have a three question Test and all questions are weighted equally; Section 1 with one correct and one incorrect answer, and Section 2 with one correct answer, the scores would be:

- Section 1 = 50%

- Section 2 = 100%

- Total Test = 2 correct / 3 incorrect = 67% (**not** (50+100)/2 = 75%)

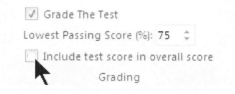

Grading

Names of Test and Section Scores

The variable names for scores are:

- *Testname*_Score
- *Sectionname*_Score

You can use these names to make things happen or display them using a Change Contents action.

Tricks of the Trade

Most people design courses such that all the content is delivered followed by a test. Sometimes, the need arises to test after each major chunk of content. You can do this in two ways.

1. You can have a series of content Chapters each followed by a graded Test and a completion Chapter. Lectora will average the scores of the tests and *weight each test equally*.

2. The second way is to have a test with a series of **Sections**. Each **Section** contains pages of content followed by questions. Lectora will score the test based on the total questions. It will *not* average the **Sections**.

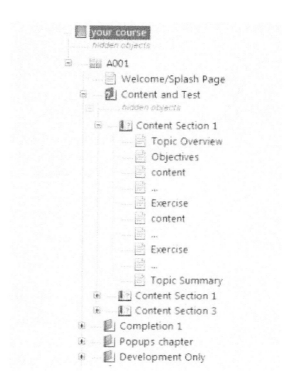

Practice What You Learned

You learned a lot about creating tests in this step. Before going on, take some time to create your own test with a couple of questions and apply these techniques. Experiment with different options. This way what you have learned will stick with you.

Remember These Key Points

Well there was a lot to learn about tests beyond just creating the questions, right?

- Best practice is to use the same (or at least very similar) navigation in the test as in the rest of the course.

- Specify the kind of results you want students to receive and use something other than your own good judgment to set the passing score.

- Make sure you have enough questions to cover each objective adequately by organizing your Test into Sections.

- Avoid giving questions different weight and partial credit. This makes is hard for learners to figure out how their tests are graded.

- If possible, give feedback when learners commit to an answer.

- Use randomizing to reduce cheating.

- Be sure your test gets graded by having an action on the last page to Process Test/Survey for non-randomized tests.

- Use a Pass/Fail Chapter to let the student know if they passed or failed, do it nicely, and let them know what to do next.

Remember, if you want the Lectora Title that I used to create this book with **working examples**, go to www.eProficiency.com/101.html.

Step 9: See How They Liked It with Surveys

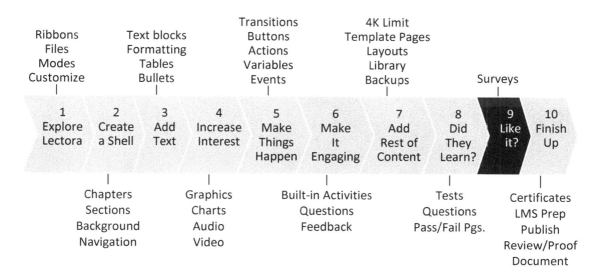

Ribbons
Files
Modes
Customize

Text blocks
Formatting
Tables
Bullets

Transitions
Buttons
Actions
Variables
Events

4K Limit
Template Pages
Layouts
Library
Backups

Surveys

| 1 Explore Lectora | 2 Create a Shell | 3 Add Text | 4 Increase Interest | 5 Make Things Happen | 6 Make It Engaging | 7 Add Rest of Content | 8 Did They Learn? | 9 Like it? | 10 Finish Up |

Chapters
Sections
Background
Navigation

Graphics
Charts
Audio
Video

Built-in Activities
Questions
Feedback

Tests
Questions
Pass/Fail Pgs.

Certificates
LMS Prep
Publish
Review/Proof
Document

In addition to determining if they learned anything, you may also want to know how the learners liked the course. This can be useful because learners who don't like the course, learn less. They may be able to suggest some improvements.

Here's what to do.

| Add a Survey | Add a survey, which is very similar to a test except the questions are not graded. |
| Get the Results | This is not always easy but you will need to figure out what works best for your organization. |

There is not a lot to say about surveys that is different from tests other than it is another way to evaluate your course. Kirkpatrick gave four levels of evaluation.

Level	Description
1. Did they like it?	This is the students' opinion about the course. It covers things like did they find it useful, entertaining, what did they like about it, what would they recommend be changed. This is where a survey comes in.
2. Did they learn anything?	This is what your tests do.
3. Did their behavior change as a result of taking the course?	This is harder to evaluate and is usually done outside the course through observation.
4. Did the change in behavior improve productivity?	This is very hard to measure because even though you can use performance measures, there could be many other things that affected performance.

Add a Survey

To add a survey to your course:

1. You click on **Survey** on the **Test & Survey** ribbon to insert one in your course.

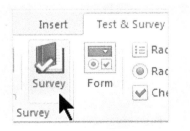

It inserts a Survey Chapter after the Chapter you were last on. If it is in the wrong place, just drag it to where you want it.

Be sure to do as you did for a Test:

- Delete the default navigation so as not to confuse learners.

- Inherit what you have in the rest of the course.

Then add the questions you want to your survey. So, what types of questions are useful here?

Probably avoid true false questions like "Did you find this course interesting?" If they answer "No", then you have not learned anything about what you need to do to make it better.

The same is true about fill in the blank.

Your better bets are Multiple-Choice and Multiple Response along with Likert questions.

Your best bets are short answer and essay because they will give you information you can use to improve the course. They are not gradable and you cannot create statistics like how many students rated the course high. Use questions like:

- "What did you like about this course?"

- "What would you change about this course?"

- If you used a Likert question, you could ask, "Why did you grade high or low?"

Get the Results

You can have the results of your survey stored on your LMS, emailed to someone, or posted elsewhere. The Email option will not work with SCORM or AICC courses.

1. On the Survey Properties ribbon in the Results Submission group, select either Custom Script or Google Drive from the custom settings.

2. Click **Settings** and enter the name of the script you want the results to go to which can either email them or store them in a database. Get your IT department to help you with this part.

Add a Completion Page

After your **Survey**, you will need somewhere for the course to go because you have two places you need to tell Lectora where it should go just like you did in a test.

Just add a page after your **Survey** to tell the learner what to do next.

Practice What You Learned

You learned about creating surveys in this step. Before going on, take some time to create your own survey and apply these techniques. Experiment with different options. Try one of each type of question you think you might use. Makes sure you can retrieve survey results. This way what you have learned will stay with you.

Remember These Key Points

- **Surveys** are very similar to **Tests** but they are not graded.
- They give you a way to identify improvements.
- It may take some work to get the results and process them.

Step 10: **Finish Your Course**

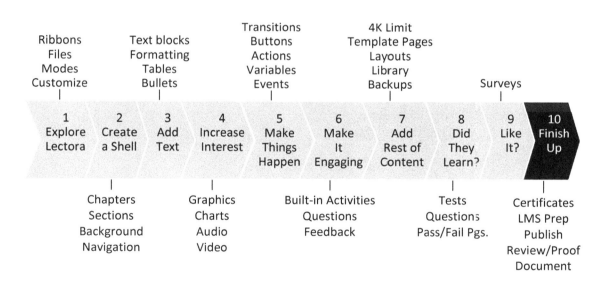

Ribbons
Files
Modes
Customize

Text blocks
Formatting
Tables
Bullets

Transitions
Buttons
Actions
Variables
Events

4K Limit
Template Pages
Layouts
Library
Backups

Surveys

| 1 Explore Lectora | 2 Create a Shell | 3 Add Text | 4 Increase Interest | 5 Make Things Happen | 6 Make It Engaging | 7 Add Rest of Content | 8 Did They Learn? | 9 Like It? | 10 Finish Up |

Chapters
Sections
Background
Navigation

Graphics
Charts
Audio
Video

Built-in Activities
Questions
Feedback

Tests
Questions
Pass/Fail Pgs.

Certificates
LMS Prep
Publish
Review/Proof
Document

This chapter brings all you have learned together to help you finish your course. It includes some things you may need to do in a number of different places, especially if you are thinking of having your learners be able to take a break from the course and come back sometime later and finish it then.

To finish up:

Do a Few Final Checks	Now that everything is in your course, you have a few critical things to check before you go public.
Add a Certificate	Some like to have a certificate the learners can print. Lectora has several standard ones or you can create your own.
Get Ready for That LMS	If you will be running your courses from an LMS, you have a few things left to do.
Publish	Select your method of publishing, select the publishing options, and publish.
Review Your Course	After publishing and removing publishing errors, do your own review and then get others to review it.
Document Your Work	If you did anything that may need explanation to the next developer or even to yourself a year from now, make a few notes before you forget.

Perform These Final Checks

1. Check the spelling in your entire document by selecting Entire Title from the dropdown list in the Spell Check option in the Review group of the Tools ribbon. You may find a few things you missed.

2. Find and replace all double spaces. This is a minor point but professional work uses only a *one* space after the punctuation at the end of a sentence. Click on Replace in the Edit group on the Home ribbon.

   This will open a dialog window where you can set a number of options and fix double spaces.

3. If you have a Test, check the Pass/Fail Chapter to be sure you have adjusted the Back button and disabled the Forward/Next button.

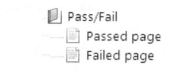

Add a Certificate Page

You can add a certificate to your course clicking on the Certificate icon in the Add More group of the Insert ribbon.

This opens a Certificate Wizard which allows you to pick from some 12 different standard certificates and then configure them using different fonts and text.

The Certificate Wizard creates a new page that has its own properties and unique page size. You can:

1. Change the background image if you don't like it.

2. Rearrange and reformat any of the text blocks.

    You will likely want to change the text a little to include the name of the course on the certificate.

The certificate page already sets the date to the current date.

Now for the tough part. The certificate page includes a text block for the student name but it is not filled in. If you are running your course from an LMS, you can access the student name from there *but* it is in "last name, first name" format. If you are not using an LMS, then you have to have students enter their name either on this page or somewhere else in the course and then use it here. Let's see how to do both of these.

Having Students Enter Their Name

Somewhere else in the course, have an entry box where students can enter their name. Then on the certificate page, use that information to populate the Student Name text block.

1. Move to the page where the students will enter their name.

2. On the **Test & Survey** ribbon, insert an **Entry Field** by clicking on the icon in the **Add Form Element** group.

3. Position it on the page and add some instructions to the student.

4. On its **Properties** ribbon, note the variable name as you will need it in just a minute.

5. In the **Initial** box, enter some text to give the learner an additional clue as to what to do.

6. Now return to the certificate page and add an action to the page.
   - Set the **Target** to the Student Name text block.
   - Set the **Value** to the name of the entry field variable.

You can use this same technique once you have the student name to personalize some pages in your course like the Passed and Failed pages.

Getting the Student Name from the LMS

If you are using an LMS, the student name is available in a reserved variable called AICC_Student_Name. And yes, that is the variable name even if you are publishing to SCORM.

Since the student name in most LMSs is stored with the last name first (Pitman,Ben), we have to add a bit of JavaScript to put it back in the right order (Benjamin Pitman). Note that this only works when published and run from an LMS where the student name is available.

1. Click on the certificate page icon in the **Title Explorer** and then on the Student Name text block.

2. Add a **Page Show** action to change the contents of the Student Name text block.

3. Click on the dropdown list in the **Value** field and select **New Variable...**

4. In the dialog window, give a name to a new variable. In our example here, we call it "_firstLastName".

The action should look like this when you are done.

Your **Title Explorer** should look like this.

At this point, we have created a variable and used it to change the name on the certificate. However, we still do not have anything in it.

5. Click again on the Student Name text block and add another action.

6. Change it to a Page Show action to Run JavaScript.

7. Click on the lower right corner of the JavaScript box and it will open a larger window for you to enter information.

8. In that window, enter this and then click OK. Note that the "{" and "}" are braces, not parentheses.

```
{
var temp =
AICC_Student_Name.getValue().split(",");
Var_firstLastName.set( temp[1] + " " +
temp[0]);
}
```

9. Click on the Conditions icon and create the following condition. This makes the AICC_Student_Name available on this page.

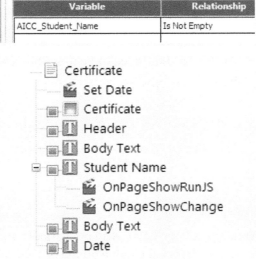

10. Click OK and you are done. Your Title Explorer for the certificate page should now look like this.

Be sure that the OnPageShowRunJS action appears *above* the OnPageShowChange action.

Get Ready for Your LMS If You Use One

If you are *not* using a Learning Management System (LMS), you can skip this part. If you are, then there are several things you need to do to prepare your course for working with an LMS. Some courses have tests and others do not. What you need to do depends a great deal on whether or not you have a Test.

Do These Things Whether or Not You Have a Test

Turn On the Assignable Unit Option

1. Begin by clicking on Title Options in the Title Setup group of the Design ribbon. This will open the following dialog window where you can set some important properties.

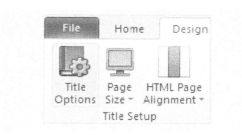

2. Select AICC/SCORM/... as the Title Type.

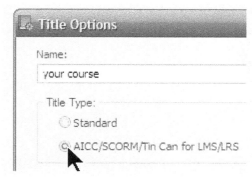

This adds an Assignable Unit (AU) to your course. The AU allows you to specify additional things needed when using an LMS.

The AU has two ribbons associated with it: Properties and Information.

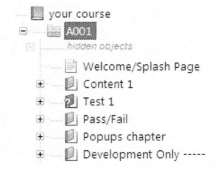

The AU **Properties** are just some global appearance characteristics (page size, HTML page alignment, background, text style, and transition). You can change the page size and alignment but I recommend you leave them the same as the Title itself (inherited).

The **Information** ribbon contains additional settings unique to an AU. Depending your LMS, the Information and Description group settings may be of use. Consult Lectora Help for more information on these.

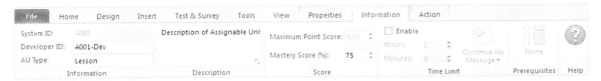

Create an Exit Button

You will need an Exit action somewhere in your course. If you don't already have one, probably the best place for one is either on the last page of content or on the passed and failed pages. Add one where it best fits your course.

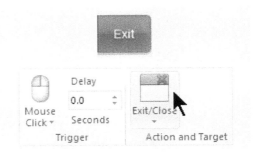

What You Need to Do If You Have a Test

If you have one or more gradable tests in your course, there are a few more things you need to do.

1. On the Results ribbon of the Test, you need to have Grade The Test checked.

2. Make sure you have *excluded* any *pretests* from the overall test score.

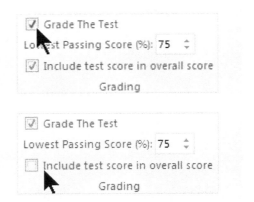

3. For non-randomized tests, make sure you have an action on the last page of the test to Process Test/Survey. See Submitting the Test for Grading on page 218.

4. One of the properties of an Assignable Unit is the Mastery Score. In the Score group on the Information ribbon, you can set the Maximum Point Score. The Lectora Help says, "Specify the maximum number of points (score) that a user can receive when completing this Title. If you leave this field blank, the program will automatically supply this value with 100 points times the total number of graded tests within the assignable unit." I guess that means in some complex LMS systems you can weight some AUs more than others based on the number of tests they have. If you don't know, leave it alone.

5. Set the Mastery Score. Each individual test has its own test score. The scores from all tests in a course are averaged together to calculate an *average test score*. If this average test score is greater than or equal to the Mastery Score, then the LMS will show learners as passed and having completed the test.

   So, if you have 2 tests and the learner passes 1 and fails 1, their average score could still be above the Mastery Score and they would pass the course. Therefore, you need to set the Mastery Score accordingly.

   – If you have just one test then set the passing score for the test and the Mastery Score *to be the same.*

   – If you have more than one test, play with the numbers in a spreadsheet so you can get the desired result. Then set your Mastery Score.

6. The Time Limit group allows you to specify the amount of time allowed for the student to take this AU. You can specify what happens when the time is up by clicking on the Continue No Message.

Warning 30: There is no easy way to display of the amount of remaining time at the AU level like there is for Tests (discussed earlier). So using this feature could surprise and frustrate the learner.

What You Need to Do If You Do *Not* Have a Test

If you don't have a test, then you don't have to worry about all that grading stuff we just covered. But, as they say, "There ain't no free lunch."

1. You might want to set the score for the course although it is not necessary in most cases. To do this, put an action on the last page to set the variable AICC_Score to the desired value.

This does not seem to apply if you are publishing for SCORM 2004.

2. Add an action to set the AICC_Lesson_Status. See the following tables for appropriate values.

Note: Settings in your LMS determine whether multiple attempts override previous values in the LMS.

Here is what you can set them to for SCORM 1.2 using the SCORM Cloud at SCORM.com.

AICC_Lesson_Status Value	LMS Completion Status	LMS Success Status
completed	complete	unknown
incomplete	incomplete	unknown
passed	complete	passed
failed	incomplete	failed

Here is what you can set them to for SCORM 2004 using the SCORM Cloud at SCORM.com.

CMI_completion_Status Value	LMS Completion Status	LMS Success Status
completed	complete	???
incomplete	incomplete	???

I do not have an AICC LMS to test on, but I know for completed at least one LMS requires a "c" instead of "completed." **If in doubt, check with your LMS support.**

Best Practice 22: Make these two actions that set the Score and the Status "OnShow" actions on the last page of the course just in case the learner chooses to close the course using the Windows® X instead of the course Exit button.

Publish Your Course

Speed Tip 13: If you are using an LMS, publish to Web (HTML) and try your course from your desktop *before* you spend time uploading and installing it on your LMS. You are likely to make changes and this will save you a good deal of time waiting for the course to upload and be recognized by the LMS.

Decide How You Will Publish

When you are finished developing your course, you will need to publish it so you can distribute it to your learners. There are many ways to publish your course. Here is a brief description of the different methods. See Lectora Help and search for "Publishing a title" for more details.

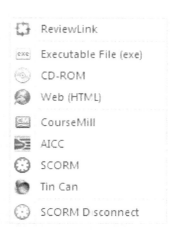

Publishing Methods

In these two publishing methods, your course will look and behave exactly like does when you are Editing it, Running it, or Previewing it in Lectora. You may not use any HTML, CSS, or JavaScript with these two methods.

Publish Method	Description
Executable File (exe)	The Executable File option will compact the entire Title and all supporting files into a single .EXE file for easy distribution. These files are only supported on the Windows® operating system.
CD-ROM	You can create a CD-ROM of your Title. When you publish to CD-ROM, Lectora creates the necessary files for you to burn to a C-ROM. After the CD-ROM is created, users will be able to insert the C-ROM into their computer's CD-ROM drive, and the published Title will automatically start. See the next topic for another way to publish to CD-ROM.

All the rest of the methods use a browser such as Internet Explorer, Google Chrome, FireFox, etc. to view the course. You can use HTML, CSS, and JavaScript with these publishing methods. Your course may appear or behave just a little differently from what it does in Lectora. Go to www.eProficiency.com/webStore/ and search for "differences" to get a free current list of these.

Publish Method	Description
ReviewLink	This method creates HTML and places it on a secure Lectora website mainly for your stakeholders to review and give feedback before going public. There are other alternatives for getting your course reviewed that are discussed later.
Web (HTML)	This method produces HTML without the wrapper code to communicate with an LMS. Use it to proof your course on your desktop. You can also put it on your server if you want run it without an LMS.
CourseMill	This option publishes your course for the CourseMill LMS from Trivantis.
AICC	Some LMS configurations require your course to be published using this method. For the latest details, see the official AICC website http://www.aicc.org.
SCORM	Most LMSs use some form of this method. SCORM stands for "Shareable Content Object Reference Model." For the latest details, see the official SCORM website http://www.adlnet.gov/.
Tin Can	Tin Can is the next step in evolution after SCORM.
SCORM Disconnect	This method allows users to use SCORM compliant courses without being connected to an LMS while the course is running.

Warning 31: Check with your IT staff to determine exactly which publishing method to use.

Alternate Way to Distribute Using a CD

If you want to use HTML, CSS, or JavaScript, then you need to view your course with a browser. You can still put the published files on a CD but you have just a little more to do. This has been tested on Windows® systems but not Mac.

1. Publish your Web (HTML).

2. Copy the html folder to the CD.

3. Using Notepad create the following two files and place them on the CD:

    Filename= **autorun.bat**
    Contents= 4 lines:

    ```
    @echo Loading CD
    @start html/index.html
    @cls
    @exit
    ```

    Filename=**autorun.inf**
    Contents=2 lines:

    ```
    [autorun]
    open=autorun.bat
    ```

4.   Burn the CD.

After the CD-ROM is created, users will be able to insert it into their computer's CD-ROM drive, and the published Title will automatically start.

Start the Publishing Process

1. Begin by clicking either the Publish icon on Quick Access Toolbar or on right of Home ribbon.

Publish

Publish

2. Click on your Publish method.

Lectora will open a Publish window and quickly error check your course. You will see a list of red and blue error messages.

- You can double-click on any message and Lectora will take you close to where the problem is.

- Blue messages are warnings. You should look them over and see if you can do something to remove them. Some can affect how your course behaves.

- Red messages are severe messages. You must fix them in order to proceed.

3. Click the Publish button at the bottom of the Publish window.

Lectora will bring up a Publish Options window. The window will change depending on which Publish method you selected.

Select Your Options

Here we will cover the most common publishing options and give you some recommendations. See Lectora Help for more details.

HTML Options Tab

This tab appears when you are publishing to some form of HTML, which includes the Web, CourseMill, AICC, SCORM, and Tin Can methods.

In the Publish area:

- Leave the Destination Folder alone. By default, Lectora will create an "html" subfolder in the same folder as your course is located.

- Select the Publish all pages option. While the Publish only updated pages option may be faster, under some rare conditions, Lectora may not publish a changed page.

- Unless you need to upload the file immediately, uncheck the Create a zip file option.

- Unless your IT staff has told you otherwise, leave the File name of first page as index.html.

In the Options area:

- Check Use Lightbox Pop Ups (this was the old Web 2.0 option). See below for Pros and Cons of this style of popups.

- Uncheck Create ALT tags for images and buttons unless you need to be 508 compliant.

- You can check Protect content if you need an additional layer of protection.

- Leave the rest of the options as they default unless your IT staff has told you otherwise.

- If you are having trouble with actions and variables, you can check the Debug Published Content option and select from several debug options. These are discussed in more detail in *Lectora 301: Techniques for Professionals*.

Pros and Cons of Lightbox Style Popup Ups

Pros	Cons
• Users encounter fewer problems with popup blockers. This is more likely to happen when you are testing from your desktop than from a server.	• The close box (X in the upper right corner) is much smaller.
• Usually only one popup window can be opened at a time. This helps keep the desk clutter down.	• If you want multiple windows open at one time, this is *not* the way to go.
• The main course (launching window) is grayed out while the popup is shown. This reduces confusion about which window is which.	• If you are using the Debugger, these do *not* stop things like OnTimer actions from running.
	• New lines are ignored. Text is just strung together. If you want new lines, you will have to publish without the Lightbox option.

JavaScript Title Manager

This and the next option are used when your course is published to some form of HTML.

☑ Use JavaScript Title Manager
☐ Include Title Manager Frame

The JavaScript Title Manager is an option you can use to free up the end user from having to install plug-ins for specific functionality like grading a test. For instance, if your Title included a test and you didn't use the JavaScript Title Manager, it would have to use a Java plug-in to store the correct answers and grade the test as the user moves from page to page. With the JavaScript Title Manager, it can place all the information for the test in an XML file and use the technology to grade the test without the user being able to view the source of each page to get the correct answer.

If you uncheck this option, the published course uses Java to accomplish these functions. Java also gives you the ability to send emails as the result of posted forms or graded tests ... you can't email from the JavaScript Title Manager so you have to uncheck this box.

Title Manager Frame

As for the Title Manager Frame, that is an option that allows the course to use a frameset to manage all the variables in the course locally without using cookies. This option is always used for SCORM and AICC publishes as no variables should ever be written to the end user's local machine. This is also a good option for HTML publishes if you have a lot of variables in the course as IE can only handle 4K for non-retained variables. If you exceed that, you could lose functionality in the course as a result of those values no longer being available to the course.

Thanks to Ed Thompson and Tim Verrelli of Trivantis

FTP Tab

You can set up the FTP tab to upload your published course to a server. While Lectora may do a fine job of this, I usually use my FTP application for this because I want to check the published file before I upload it. Once checked, I don't want to have to republish it.

Compress and Convert Tab

This tab can make your courses run faster over a network. Low compression settings result in higher quality but larger file sizes. Higher compression settings will result in lower quality and smaller file sizes. This means the courses should run faster over a network. Experiment with different settings to get the files as small as possible and yet have acceptable quality.

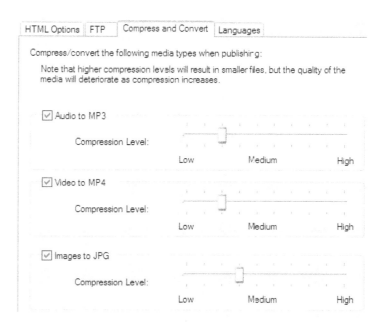

Speed Tip 14: When you select these compression options, Lectora compresses audio, video, and images *every* time you publish. This may cause your publishing process to take a long time (like 5-10 minutes). Most courses should publish in under a minute. If yours takes longer than that, see if it is compressing any objects (watch the publishing messages). If so, make note of them. Then locate these resources in the **Resource Manager** and compress them *once* there by clicking on them and clicking the **Convert to MP4/MP3** button. This can greatly speed up publishing.

Languages Tab

If you need to have your course published in several languages, then the **Language** tab can be of some help. Before it is of use, you have to translate the course and the built-in messages that can appear like "Your test results have been submitted".

1. On the Tools ribbon, use the Translations tool to export all the course text except for the built-in messages. Translate your text and reimport. See the Appendix 2: Translation Tips for more details. Put the translation file in a folder by itself and note its name.

2. To translate the built-in messages, on the File menu, select Preferences and in the Publish Strings area:

   – Click Add to give a name to the translated strings.

   – Export the Default Publish Strings to the translation file folder.

   – Outside Lectora, translate them using NotePad or MS WordPad.

   – Back in Lectora in the Publish Strings area, select that name in the String Set area and Import them.

Now you are ready to use the Languages tab.

3. In the New Language area, select your Translation File, Publish String Set, and the Publish Folder.

4. Click Add Language and your new language will appear in the bottom box.

Now, when you publish, Lectora will publish a different version of the course for the default language and each language listed on this tab and place the published files in the folders you specified. These can be found inside the html folder in Windows®.

Executable Options

If you elected to publish as an Executable File, on the Executable Options tab, specify the published output folder and file name.

- You can replace the icon if you wish by checking that option and specifying the location of the icon.

- You can have the published file password protected by checking that box and entering a password.

CD Options

If you elected to publish using CD-ROM option, you can specify the destination folder.

- Leave the Destination Folder alone. By default, Lectora will create an "cd" subfolder in the same folder as your course is located.

- Select the Publish all pages option. While the Publish only updated pages option may be faster, under some rare conditions, Lectora may not publish a changed page.

- Uncheck the Create a zip file option because zipped CD files will not run when zipped. You might use this option if you were going to send the file to someone who was then going to unzip and burn some CDs.

- You can replace the icon if you wish by checking that option and specifying the location of the icon.

CourseMill Options

Here you can enter the Course ID, the Instructor ID, and Password for the CourseMill LMS.

SCORM Options

If you are publishing to SCORM, on this tab, you begin by specifying the SCORM Conformance Level. Check with your LMS technical staff to determine which level to use and the other SCORM settings.

If you check the Prompt the user to navigate to the last viewed page, you can change the text that is displayed by going to the File menu > Preferences > Publish Strings and look for this. You can change the highlighted text to be what you would prefer.

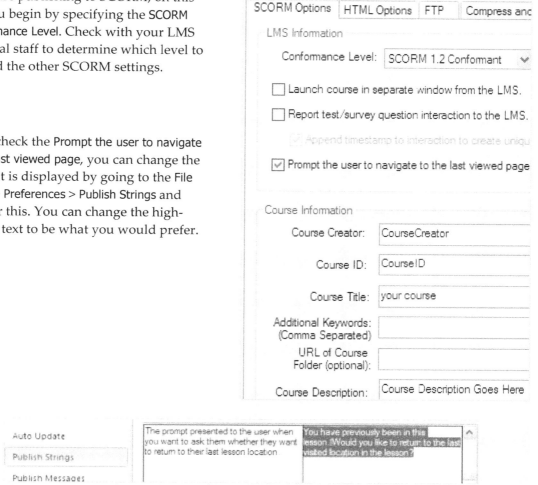

If you want to change the format of the window, you have to use an advanced technique covered in *Lectora 301: Techniques for Professional*.

Finish the Publishing

Click on the Publish button at the bottom of the window. Lectora will publish the course.

If there are any serious errors, they will be shown in red. You can click on them and Lectora will take you where the problem is. You must fix the red errors before you can proceed.

Review Your Course

If your publishing took longer than a minute, there may be audio or video files that are being compressed during publishing. See the Compress and Convert Tab topic on page 243.

Once the publishing is complete, you should run through your course to be sure everything still looks right and works right. Click the Preview button at the bottom of the Publish window. If you have more than one browser installed, you can select a browser from the dropdown list.

Make Sure Everything Looks and Works Right

At last count there were some 40 differences between the way things looked and worked in Run or Preview mode and when published to HTML. You can go to www.eProficiency.com/webStore/ and search for "differences" to get a free current list of these.

Before you upload your course to a server, you should make a pass through your course.

If you are publishing to any form of HTML and your learners will use a browser to view your course, you should check every page to make sure they look right. Make sure:

- Objects still line up
- All text is showing and does not overlap nearby objects
- No unexpected characters show up
- All actions still work as expected

 Warning 32: Not all browsers are equal. If your target audience may be using different browsers, you should check your course in each one of them because some things may look different or behave differently.

Decide What Technology You Will Use to Get Reviewer Feedback

Once you are satisfied with your course, you need to get it reviewed by some of your stakeholders. You need to give them access to the published course. You will also need to give them instructions on what you want them to do and when you want their feedback.

Begin by deciding which technology you will use. There are several different ways you can use to have reviewers report issues. A lot depends on how physically close you are to the reviewer, technology preferences and capabilities of the reviewers, expected number of issues, and of course your preferences.

Technique	Description
Print the Problem Page and Mark Up	If you are physically close to the reviewer and expect minimal changes (like this is the third review), then probably the easiest approach is for them to simply print the page on paper, mark it up, and hand it to you.
Using ReviewLink or Similar Tool	Publish your course selecting the ReviewLink option. Your course is uploaded the Trivantis ReviewLink website. You can then give a link to your reviewers. They can enter review notes in special areas as they review the course.
MS Word® Document	They can simply make notes in a MS Word® document identifying the page and issue and send that to you. You can copy and paste changed text into Lectora. Be sure to Paste Unformatted.
MS Word® Table with Page Names	You can create a MS Word® document with the names of the pages to make it a little easier. You could do this by copying the text from a Table of Contents and pasting it into MS Word® and formatting it for them.
Exporting the Text Using the Translation Tool	You can use the Translation tool and export all the text to an RTF document. They can make changes to the text and you can reimport it. This can be a big time saver because you do *not* have to copy and paste the changes. See Appendix 2: Translation Tips for more details. The reviewers *must* use a tool like WordPad, *not* MS Word®.
Exporting the Text to MS Word®	You can export the text to MS Word® and give them that file to make changes in. Where possible, arrange the text blocks *in the* Title Explorer in the sequence you want to see them in MS Word®. Where they appear on the page has *nothing* to do with the sequence in which they appear in the Word® document. For example, even though your page title text block is positioned at the top of the page, if it is below the body text block in the Title Explorer, the exported file will show the body text first and *then* the title.
Printing Your Pages from Lectora	You can also print your course to paper. Pick one of layouts from the list shown when you go to print. Note that the Outline format does *not* print the text on the page, just an outline similar to the Title Explorer. Text blocks filled in by actions like Breadcrumbs will *not* show. Objects can be suppressed from printing by hiding them using the visibility check boxes just to the left of the object in the Title Explorer.

Give Instructions to Reviewers

If you just give vague instructions to your reviewers like, "Please review this course and let me know what you find" you are *not* likely to get a very thorough review. It is better to give them specific instructions as to what to look for and how to report problems. Your instructions should include:

- When response is needed
- What to look for
- How to report issues

Tell Them When Response Is Needed

Don't leave this to chance. I can't tell you the number of times teams I have worked with have sent out requests for review and then complained that people are not reviewing. When I ask if they gave a time frame, the complainers almost always answer, "No. I thought it was obvious." Well it is *not*. When you contact your reviewers:

- Tell them how long it will likely take (allow at least one minute per page, more if you have complex pages, audio, or video).
- Tell them exactly *when* you need their response.
- Ask them to confirm that they will be able to meet the schedule.

Tell Them What to Look For

Not everyone is good at catching all kinds of errors or problems. Some people are better at one kind of thing and not so good at others. Here is list of some different kinds of reviewers and what you could have them focus on. Clearly one person may be able to do several of these reviews.

Reviewer	What to Have Them Focus On
Corporate Communications dept.	• Does it comply with corporate guidelines for use of colors, fonts, logo?
Legal dept.	• Is it legally correct?
Language major	• Look for spelling, grammar, and word usage errors. • Was translation correct?
Graphic artist	• Are there any improvements needed in page layout? • Are pictures treated correctly and uniformly?

Reviewer	What to Have Them Focus On
Trainer/instructional designer	• Is this good e-learning design? • Is all the content covered that was in the storyboard? • Are the objectives well framed? • Are the exercises well worded exercises and give good feedback?
Subject matter expert (SME)	• Are all key points covered? • Is any content missing? • Is everything worded properly?
Your boss	• What do you think? (There will almost always be something he/she wants to change.)
Sponsor	• Is this what he/she expected?
Technical person	• Do all the buttons work? • Do all the communications with email or LMS work and the completion status work properly? • Does the course resume properly?
Typical learner on their computer	• Does everything work? • Are instructions for exercises clear? • Does it respond quickly enough (bandwidth issues)? • Did you have any problems with the course? • Was anything confusing or unclear?

Tell Them How to Report Issues

Explain the technology you are using for them to report problems and changes—email, ReviewLink, etc.

Document What You Did

People who are new to Lectora tend to ignore any kind of documentation. Once they see how to do something, it all seems obvious. However, experience has shown that this is not true. The original author leaves and the next developer has a hard time understanding just what is going on.

While it is not necessary to document everything, you can make your course easier to maintain if you:

- Use meaningful object names in the Title Explorer.
- Use friendly variable names and values.
- Use Notes.
- Use object Descriptons.
- Use hidden text blocks

Write Notes

You can add notes to pages. Notes do not appear to the learner and are not part of the package when you publish your course. Notes can be color coded and you can produce a report listing all the Notes in your course.

Add a Note to any page in your course by:

- clicking on the Add Note icon in the Review group on the Tools ribbon or

- right clicking on the page and select Add a note or

- setting up a keyboard shortcut by right clicking on a ribbon and selecting Customize.

A Note icon will appear on your page. You can change the color of the note by right clicking on it and selecting Note Color.

You can have several Notes on a page and you can drag them to be near the object(s) they refer to.

Notes in a course are easy to find and are a great way to leave reminders to yourself. The Page name on pages with notes becomes bold italic as well as the containing Section and Chapter.

If you want a quick list of all the Notes in your course, you can produce a Notes Report using the icon in the Review group on the Tools ribbon.

Use Object Descriptions

A feature introduced in Lectora 11 is the object Description.

In the lower right of either the Properties ribbon or the Action ribbon is a diagonal arrow. Clicking on it opens a description window where you can enter pretty much anything you like to describe the object. This is especially handy for:

- Complex actions

- HTML objects (covered in *Lectora 301: Techniques for Professionals*)

Use Hidden Text Blocks

The final way to document things is to put a text block on the page that stands out (maybe has a different background color) and is Initially Hidden. I use this technique in one course where there are two different ways to publish the course and the instructions are in a text block like this on the very first page. If anyone else picks up the course using Lectora, they immediately know the different settings to publish it.

Practice What You Learned

In this step, you learned what you must do to finish your course. Take some time to apply these techniques. Experiment with different options. This way what you have learned will stay with you.

Remember **These** Key Points

You may think you were done but wait. You may still need to:

- Do a final check on your Test and Pass/Fail Chapters, spell check, and remove double spaces.

- Make a few changes to get ready to communicate with an LMS.

- There are many differences between how a course appears and behaves in Lectora compared to how it does when viewed through a browser.

- You can only use HTML objects, CSS, and JavaScript with courses that will be viewed using a browser, not with courses published to Executable files.

- No one person is good at catching all the different kinds of potential problems. Use multiple reviewers with different specialties.

- Pick a reviewer-friendly way to review your course.

- Give your reviewers clear instructions on how to access the course, how to use the reviewing technique, what to focus on, how long to expect it to take, and when you need their review.

- Document what you did.

Remember, if you want the Lectora Title that I used to create this book with **working examples**, go to www.eProficiency.com/101.html.

Appendix 1: LMS Error Messages or Problems

LMSSetValue Error: Data Model Element Type Mismatch

If you get this, your action to set the LMS status variable is incorrect. See What You Need to Do If You Do *Not* Have a Test on page 236.

LMSSetValue Error: Incorrect Data Type

If you get this, your action to set the LMS status variable is incorrect. See What You Need to Do If You Do *Not* Have a Test on page 236.

Some of the persistent data was not able to be stored

Possible known causes:

- You may have too much data being sent to the LMS. Compare how much data you are sending to the LMS (retained variables) to how much can be stored. See Adapt to the 4K Hidden Limit on page 179.

- This is a message that the course produces when it passes a variable to the LMS' API adapter using a LMSSetValue() command and *compares* that with what it gets back from the API with a LMSGetValue() command. Somehow the data is being sent to the LMS and being changed before it comes back to be verified. **If you have an On Show Go To or On Show Exit action on a page, give it a delay of .5to 1sec. This frequently fixes the problem.**

Close Button Does Not Close Window Properly.

Make sure you have the publish option "The published course will be presented in a separate window than the LMS" checked.

Course Freezes as It Loads

Make sure you have the Use JavaScript Title Explorer option on the Options tab checked when you publish.

Unknown

From one of the users on the Lectora Community forum:"Lately we prepared a test in one of our course and it worked fine in English but French users kept getting an error message. After discussion with our consultant developer about the fact that the problem resided with the French language I remembered having a language problem last year when we found that Lectora files with French accents would not be uploaded in our LMS. So working from this we discovered that although we can translate the values True or False into Vrai ou Faux, Lectora does not recongnize it as a valid variable and keeps looking for it when we submit the test. The work around was then to identify the type of question as a Multiple Choice option with Vrai ou Faux being the possible answers. It now works fine. Regards, Pierrette Blanchette"

Appendix 2: Translation Tips

The Translation tool exports the text in the course to an RTF file. That file can now be modified and the new text will can be imported either permanently or just when you publish the course.

You can use this can use this capability in several ways.

- You can use it to permanently translate a course. You make a copy of the course and import the translated text into it and publish from there. This technique allows you to examine the translated course before publishing and make sure the text blocks did not expand too much and overlap other things on the page.

- You can use it to translate your course at just Publish time using the Languages tab when you publish.

- You can use it to quickly make mass changes in a course rather than use the Lectora Find and Replace which takes a while for long courses.

- You can have reviewers make text changes which saves you having to copy and paste all the changes.

 Warning 33: There can be problems using this tool. If you have created two-line text buttons, sometimes they do not look quite right after import even if you made *no* changes. To avoid problems, before you do anything, copy your course Title file (AWT file) to be safe. Then export your text and immediately import it. Now quickly page through your course from beginning to end checking things. Make sure all still looks right, especially buttons. You can use the Page Down key to do this. Then publish to HTML and check that version. If all still looks right, proceed with translation.

Before Translation Prepare Your Title

While developing the original course:

1. Where possible, arrange the text blocks *in the* Title Explorer in the sequence you want to see them in the exported file. Where they appear on the page has *nothing* to do with how they are

exported. For example, even though your page title text block is positioned at the top of the page, if it is below the body text block in the Title Explorer, the exported file will show the body text first and *then* the title.

2. Don't use the ability to set the contents of a text block by using an action because translation export does not export this text.

3. Do not click on a text block and center it or apply any kind of formatting to it (indents, bullets, etc.). Instead, click inside the text block, select the desired text, and format as desired. Formatting applied to the box as a whole may be lost when the translated text is imported later.

4. If you are using a Table of Contents or actions that use the names of the Chapter, Section, or page in the Title Explorer, be sure you check the box to include them. This will make it harder to maintain if you are responsible for changes in the translated version and do not read the language.

5. Make text blocks a little higher than needed to allow for expansion. While there is an option to have that done for you on import, it does not move other objects that may now overlap the text block.

6. Use Verdana font as it usually does not ends up a little smaller when published to HTML as opposed to Arial, which usually expands over-running the text blocks.

7. Avoid putting objects in text blocks. They end up at the beginning of the box instead of where they were.

8. Avoid tables if you can help it. You would be amazed how much you depend on words being the right size. If you do use tables, flag the pages using Notes and be sure to check them after importing the translated file.

9. Avoid Flash objects that contain text as there is no easy way to translate them. This includes the animated Flash activities that come with Lectora.

10. Buttons created with the Button Wizard are translated. Buttons included with the Title Wizards are *not*. If your button text expands, you may have to manually adjust your buttons.

11. Avoid using white text because it is very hard to see in WordPad because you can't see the white text on a white background.

Export the Text

1. In Lectora, click on the Translations icon. This will open a Translation Manager dialog window.

2. Click Export text and the Include Image and Button names options. If you are using actions to display Chapter, Section, or Page names or a Table of Contents, check that option.

3. You can change the location of the translation file but I recommend that you leave it alone for now so you are sure you know where to find it.

4. Then click OK at the bottom of the window. Lectora creates an RTF file in the same folder as your course Title is. The file will include text that must not be altered. This text is displayed in red and is similar to this: ##~~Do not edit this line. 999~~##

Now your course is ready for translation. Note that any words in graphics will *not* be exported. You will need to modify them with your graphics editor.

Translate Your Text

1. Use WordPad, *not* MS Word®. It reduces possible the introduction of unnecessary characters. I have tried several times to use MS Word® and the results are always disastrous. MS Word® introduces hidden characters which show up after import or sometimes not until the course is published to HTML.

2. Sometimes you will need to do something special to translate links and retain the URL. Suppose you had "Click here for more info" to translate as a link.

    – Replace first replace the letter from the second to the next to last = "lick here form more inf",

    – then replace the "C" at the beginning, and

    – then the "o" at the end. This keeps the link from being destroyed.

3. Open the translated file in WordPad and look it over. If you find paragraphs with 1), 2), etc in front of them, change to bullets or know you will have to fix in Lectora. It is easier to change them here.

4. If your translator did use MS Word® and you ended up with curly quotes, apostrophes, and long dashes, replace them with straight quotes, apostrophes, and short dashes.

Import the Translated Text

1. Before you import, be sure you have made a copy of your course just in case something goes wrong.

2. Back in Lectora, click on the Translations icon again.

3. Select the Increase text block size option.

4. Immediately check the size of the new .awt file. I had one go from 2MB to 30MB. If yours expanded by several meg, try this. Many people have had success with it.
   - Back up one step and open the translated RTF file in MS WordPad.
   - Click in front of the first character and then scroll down to the last line, hold the Shift key down and click just before the last character.
   - Copy.
   - Create a *new* RTF document and paste.
   - Retype the last character.
   - Save.
   - Import this file into Lectora as the translated file.

   No, I don't know why this works but it does. Your new file size will be fairly close to the old one.

Check the Course After Import

Check the course both in Edit mode as well as when published to HTML.

1. Start on the last page and work up so you don't have to keep scrolling down to get more pages. The expanded pages will scroll off the bottom of the left pane. You can use the Page Up key to do this.

2. Fill-in-the-blank questions need to be checked again to be sure the correct answer is recognized and for *length*.

3. If you had objects in text blocks, they end up at the front of the box instead of where they were. Find those boxes and repair.

4. Check *bullets* - sometimes they seem to get dropped or are too small.

5. Check centering of text. Sometimes this ends up left justified. The cause seems to be applying centering to the text block instead of to the paragraphs within the text block.

6. Look for text built with actions such as page numbering that still needs to be translated.

7. Publish to HTML and review. Many times things look fine in Lectora but not when published, especially the lines beginning with 0), 1) , etc. mentioned above. If you do, go to the text block, copy all the text, cut, paste back *unformatted*, and reformat.

8. Remember that you can import the same text more than once. If you find changes would be easier to the RTF file, you can go back and make them and then re-import.

9. If you find that some text blocks are too big and no amount of adjusting the layout will fix the problem, drop the font size down one point.

Translate Publish Strings

Unfortunately you are not quite done. There are many messages that Lectora uses when things happen in the course such as the default correct and incorrect feedback messages, messages telling the student their scores on test, and many more. These are all stored in the Published Strings area of Preferences on the File menu.

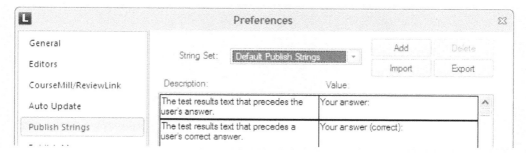

These need to be translated too.

1. Click Add and give your new string set a name.

2. Export them. Be sure you note where it is putting the output file. I usually change it to be the same folder as my Lectora Title.

3. Translate the text.

4. Back in Lectora, select that string set from the dropdown list and then import the new string set.

Multiple Courses or One Course

After having done several of these, I personally recommend that you copy the course, translate it, and have two options the learner can select from on the LMS.

If your boss/client insists on both versions in the same Title, then these tips are for you.

- Copy the .awt file.

- Translate it.

- Change the name of all the variables that are unique to the translated version like question numbers. Do something like add "_spa" if you were doing a translation to Spanish. Why? Because when, in a later step, you copy these pages back into the English Title, all the actions connected to the variables will remain in tact. Otherwise you will have a big mess.

- Copy all Chapters in the translated Title and paste into the original Title.

- If you need to, you may need to create some new graphics with translated words on them.

Lectora – English Dictionary

Lectora	English	English Definition
AICC	AICC	A set of standards for an LMS communicating with a course set by the Aviation Industry CBT Committee. It is less commonly used than SCORM.
BMP	Windows bitmap	A file format for graphics. See About Image File Types on page 75.
DPI	dots per inch	Also referred to as PPI (pixels per inch). The resolution of a graphic in dots per inch. For printing the more dots per inch, the better the quality. However, on a computer, you don't need anything higher than 96PPI because that is all they currently display. Windows® systems use 96PPI while Macs use 72PPI.
GIF	Graphic Image File	See About Image File Types on page 75.
HTML	browser used by browsers	The language used by internet browsers like Internet Explorer, Google Chrome, etc. to create web pages.
icon	little graphic thingie	An image representing something. In the Lectora interface, these are used like buttons.
inherit	things on the page that come from master pages	Inheritance allows you to put objects like the navigation buttons, logos, background graphics at a higher level such as the Title or Chapter level and they are "inherited" by all the "children" (Chapters, Sections, Pages) under them.
JPG	picture file	A graphics image file type. See About Image File Types on page 75.
layering	which thing is in front	The concept referring to which objects are in front of other objects on the page when stacked.
LMS	computer system that delivers courses to	Learning Management System. This is where most e-learning courses are launched from. They control who has access to what courses, record course progress, and course completion.

	students	
navigate	move around	To move around within the course using buttons, menus, or tables of contents.
object	thing	Anything you have in your course. It includes an image, a text block, a group, a video, an audio file, a Page, a Chapter, or even an action.
pixel	little tiny point on the screen	A single point on a computer screen. Windows uses 96 dots per inch while Macs use 72 dots per inch.
PNG	another kind of picture file	A graphics image file type. See About Image File Types on page 75.
pcint	font size	A mysterious size measurement used for fonts. The same word in different fonts but the same font size can be a different physical size.

Mysterious	12pt Palatio Linotype
Mysterious	12pt Verdana
Mysterious	12pt Arial

PPI	pixels per inch	Also referred to as DPI (dots per inch). The resolution of a graphic in dots per inch. For printing the more dots per inch, the better the quality. But on a computer, you don't need anything higher than 96PPI because that is all they currently display. Windows systems use 96PPI while Macs use 72PPI.
properties	options, characteristics, attributes	Characteristics or attributes of an item (object) in your course like the size, position, color, … Most properties are options that you can set.
resolution	how much can show on your monitor	Can refer to the width and height of your computer monitor in pixels. The more the better. It also can refer to DPI/PPI.
RGB	red-green-blue	A three color method (red, green, blue) used to define a given color using numbers between 0 (none) and 255 (maximum) for each color. 0,0,0 is black, 255,0,0 is red, 128,128,128 is medium gray, etc.
SCORM	SCIRM	Sharable Content Object Reference Model. Currently the most common set of standards for an LMS communicating with a course.

Index